# SPEAKING TO THINK
# THINKING TO SPEAK

# SPEAKING TO THINK
# THINKING TO SPEAK

## The Importance of Talk in the Learning Process

### VIRGINIA O'KEEFE, PH.D.

Boynton/Cook Publishers
HEINEMANN
Portsmouth, NH

Boynton/Cook Publishers Inc.
A subsidiary of Reed Elsevier Inc.
361 Hanover Street
Portsmouth, NH 03801-3912
*Offices and agents throughout the world*

Every effort has been made to contact the copyright holders for permission to reprint borrowed material where necessary. We regret any oversights that may have occurred and would be happy to rectify them in future printings of this work.

The author and publisher wish to thank those who granted permission to reprint previously published material:

Excerpts from *Meaning and Mind: An Intrapersonal Approach to Human Communication* by Leonard Shedletsky. © 1989 by the Speech Communication Association. Reprinted by permission of the publisher.

Excerpts from *Quiet Children and the Classroom Teacher*, Second Edition, by James C. McCroskey and Virginia P. Richmond. © 1991 by the Speech Communication Association. Reprinted by permission of the publisher.

Library of Congress Cataloging-in-Publication Data

O'Keefe, Virginia P.
    Speaking to think/thinking to speak: the importance of talk in the learning process
      p.  cm.
    Includes bibliographical references
    ISBN 0-86709-358-7  (acid-free paper)
    1. Language arts (Secondary)  2. Oral communication—Study and
teaching (Secondary)  3. Thought and thinking—Study and teaching
(Secondary)  4. Learning.  I. Title.
LB1631.054  1995
428'.0071'2—dc20                                 94-45175
                                                   CIP

Editor: Robert Boynton
Production: CTG Publishing Services, Camden, Maine
Cover design: Darci Mehall
Cover photograph: Elaine Rebman

Printed in the United States of America on acid-free paper
04 03 02 01     DA 6 5 4 3

*To my children
and their families*

# Contents

· · · · · · · · · · · · · · · · · · · ·

# *Preface*

· · · · · · · · · · · · · · · · · · · · · · · ·

I called this book *Speaking to Think/Thinking to Speak* to empha-
size the importance of talk in the learning process. We know
what we know when we say it. James Britton speaks of this
phenomenon as shaping thought at the point of utterance.
Since speaking to ourselves and others is the primary way we
learn throughout our lives, when we exclude classroom talk, or
minimize its influence, we handicap our learners. Research
indicates that sharing information, processing knowledge, and
expressing thoughts aloud help all learners to think better and
to achieve more academically.

While talking to learn is not a new idea in education, spoken
language receives diminishing attention as children advance
through the grades. Talk becomes transparent. It is the way
we do things, not what is consciously done. But we need to
look carefully *at* talk, not just *through* it, if we are to enhance
students' thinking. We need to synthesize language arts, education psychology, and communication studies in order to
understand talk and its effect on learning. Although speaking
for thinking should be practiced and taught in every subject at
every level of education, for the most part oral language, no
less than written, will be primarily taught in English classes, if
it is taught at all. For that reason, middle and secondary school
language arts teachers play a strategic role in the development
of oral abilities and their corresponding thinking skills. Ignor-
ing oral language, or equating the spoken word to the written
one, shortchanges a key developmental process. Yet study after
study reveals that most classrooms currently depend on
teacher-centered expository communication, instead of a form
of student-centered shared communication.

*Speaking to Think/Thinking to Speak* provides a new look at talk in the classroom by explaining its value, showing how it works, and offering practical suggestions to make it successful. The ideas and suggestions contained in this book are a product of more than twenty years of teaching English, Speech, Forensics, and Debate in secondary school, plus considerable time spent teaching college communication courses. Through this experience, I observed an apparent connection between students' improvement in writing and thinking when they became more proficient speakers. My curiosity about a possible link between speaking and thinking led me to New York University's doctoral program and courses of study under James Britton and others in Oxford, England. My research continued in my own classroom and those of other teachers who generously shared their time and explorations. The kinds of understandings that students develop when they own the process seem to have a profound effect on their development. Several students whose work is included in this text vividly remember their discussions from almost a decade ago and still recall the perceptions that they and their classmates jointly formed.

These students' voices, through transcripts and writings, illustrate the process of talking to think. Their informal journals reflect what happened as they shaped thoughts with language. Rather than causing confusion, speech creates clarity. Why is talk so effective? It seems that talk allows students to begin where they are and grow to what they can be. We do not understand or know something until we can shape it to fit our experience. On the other hand, we can expand our ideas through the shared experiences of a community of learners, or what Vygotsky called the zone of proximal development. Discovering knowledge in this way not only taps the zone but also makes the knowledge gained more lasting.

Reading this book should provide an increased appreciation for the value of talk in the language arts classroom. However, the major advantage is a repertoire of manageable ways to increase students' active participation in communication without a corresponding loss of classroom control. Although students are talking, the emphasis in both theory and practice is on their responsibility to listen, share, and produce results. Of special interest to classroom teachers are the following topics.

1. Ways to facilitate whole class discussion
2. Practical guides to develop student leadership
3. Strategies to improve student questioning
4. Small group discussion techniques especially appropriate for English classrooms
5. Solving problems with reluctant speakers
6. Authentic speaking and listening assessments
7. The role of listening in the learning process with suggestions for both the teacher and students
8. Numerous activities to encourage speaking and listening as part of the learning process
9. Suggested questions for teacher-researchers to pursue

Especially noteworthy are the concerns not usually discussed in current literature. For example, communication fear is a reality, and its effect can be crippling. The absence of oral work in a classroom and its distrust may be a reflection of a teacher's own fears or discomfort with this mode of expression. A frank examination of communication apprehension (CA), as communication scholars call it, reveals possible barriers to using speech in the classroom for both the teacher and the students.

Placing the teacher in the role of listener and the student in the role of questioner reverses the traditional approach to teaching. However, teachers can relinquish the front of the room without abandoning control. The difference is in providing a scaffold for thought that allows learners to construct their knowledge. The ways we learn are as important as the facts that we acquire. Joining the two processes is the business of language arts classrooms since languaging is the heart of thought.

Underlying the theory and practice described is my belief in the teacher as the expert. I do not advocate a top-down methodology. Each teacher needs to become his or her own theorist as well as practitioner through personal research in the classroom. Keeping journals, making assessments, designing instruments, monitoring progress, and welcoming observations are ways we can build our knowledge about learning. Mistakes are opportunities for growth. We, no less than students, must be ready to take risks. Our documentation aids a field too little explored and too greatly exploited.

Some final words about the design of this book should assist the reader. Teachers are busy people with diverse needs and interests. For those who want practical, hands-on descriptions of classroom activities, I recommend reading Chapter 3, "The Questioning Class"; Chapter 4, "Whole Class Discussion"; Chapter 5, "Cooperative Learning and Small Groups"; Chapter 6, "Communication and Reader Response"; and Chapter 7, "Searching for Authentic Assessment." Those who are more interested in the theory and research underlying this teaching method should read Chapter 1, "Speaking to Think," and Chapter 2, "Teaching for Discovery." Or the reader can randomly select topics of interest, since each chapter can be read independently. In addition, the activities listed at the end of every chapter are multifaceted. While they are selected to illustrate individual chapter subjects, they are versatile enough to support any instructional program.

I think of this book as a beginning. It is my hope that *Speaking to Think/Thinking to Speak* will encourage teachers to listen to the speakers in their classrooms with new awareness and greater understanding. Building ideas together in an environment of trust is a demanding but rewarding journey. The road maps are still being written. Teachers, as researchers, are the cartographers.

# *Acknowledgments*

· · · · · · · · · · · · · · · · · · · ·

This book began a dozen years ago in my classroom as I questioned how talking and thinking might be connected. Those questions led me on a discovery journey spanning thousands of miles and involving hundreds of people, mostly my students. I wish I could acknowledge each person who contributed ideas and assistance, but that is impossible in this limited space. Nevertheless, there are some individuals who must be recognized specifically. First of all, I was privileged to study under Jimmy Britton in my doctoral program at New York University. From him I gained important insights about the significance of oral language and its influence on our development of concepts. Jimmy also encouraged me, a neophyte researcher, to write my first book. Gordon Pradl and Damien Martin directed my research at critical moments, helping me to define my aims. John Mayher provided valuable theoretical and practical advice about the value of oral response in the classroom, demonstrating its efficacy with his own style of teaching. Don Boileau helped to refine my ideas about communication and its place in learning.

However, for the most important influence, I have to credit Harold Vine, who through his patience and vision shaped the future of my teaching. He modeled for me the roles of responder, teacher, and evaluator as we worked together to find meaningful ways to interpret classroom communication. It was from Harold that I learned that examining the ordinary can yield extraordinary insights.

My mentors included colleagues who allowed me to visit their classrooms, especially Cecelia Blotkamp and Rena McCune. Marian Mohr helped me to look at my own classroom with the eyes of a researcher-observer as well as a teacher.

Her reading of the manuscript sharpened the focus and clarified the message. Diane Grainer, Kathryn Schweers, and Kim O'Keefe also read portions of the manuscript, suggesting valuable ideas for revision.

A major contribution to this book are the examples of students' classroom talk and writing. I am grateful that I have the chance to share their words with others. Though their names have been changed to fictitious ones, nevertheless the thoughts expressed remain uniquely theirs.

Timothy Wells' coaching and advice were vital in the initial stages of this book. His recommendations for form and focus were instrumental in its design. And the final text has been shaped by the insightful comments and painstaking attention to details by my editor, Peter Stillman. His support and confidence in the product made the task easier.

Pat Goll prepared most of the classroom transcripts. Christine Rainwater and Eleanor Bernier offered encouragement as they helped with word processing.

I especially thank my husband, James O'Keefe, for being a patient listener, copy editor, and supporter through the years it has taken to explore this topic and complete the book.

# SPEAKING TO THINK
# THINKING TO SPEAK

# ● *One*

. . . . . . . . . . . . . . . . . . .

## *Speaking to Think*

> I tell my kids that only 5 percent of the people think, and then 10 percent think they think, and 85 percent of the people prefer to die before [they] think . . . If we could teach our kids how to think, how to communicate—we'd have the job done.
>
> —*Escalante*

Schools have been designed to meet the needs of a certain class of learners—those for whom passivity is an acceptable way of learning. Quiet classrooms with docile students, dominated by the teacher's voice, are still perceived as "good" classrooms. That method works well for a little over a third of our student population. What about the rest? Some learn passivity to their detriment—they stop asking questions for fear of looking "stupid." Some withdraw and become "shy." Others are drugged in order to "fit in." And others resist the regime: talk when they are supposed to listen, and walk around when they are supposed to sit, ask questions, or make comments. We call those children "misfits," and label them "at-risk." They frequent the principal's office, they have babies as teenagers, they drop out to work in the local factories. We know—and *they* know—they will never make it in our little red schoolhouse. These kids are America's throwaways.

Statistics may tell us what schools are doing well or not, but all of us as teachers know that we are losing some of our children each year. If they are not in our own classrooms, we can see potential dropouts in the halls or on the playground. To do less well than they are able is also a loss. Even if the score card says we are doing all right by the average student, as some reports indicate, those students may be shortchanged. The aspiring architect settles on being a file clerk. The potential engineer slides into an assembly-line spot. Too many dreams turn to chalk dust. The practical-minded might say, "Just as well. We wouldn't have enough professional jobs if all those kids followed through."

Idealists, as teachers must be, believe that regardless of the job market each person should develop to his or her maximum ability. That is what teaching is all about. If we wanted only the minimum result, we would not last long in a demanding profession. It is our dreams that keep us going long after the last bell, after the last bus has left. We believe that kids can *do* and kids can *grow*, and that is what we want for them.

I began my first book, *Affecting Critical Thinking Through Speech*, with these words:

> When I walk into my classroom every day, I realize I am sur-rounded by twenty to thirty highly energized people—my students. They are fueled and set to soar if I can but find the right button to push. The challenge never ends. (1988a, 1)

One of my fellow teachers chided me after reading this. He said I must have been writing about a different school. He had the same students and they were lifeless clods. That set me to thinking. What does "turn on" a student to learning? If most of my colleagues viewed students as passive sponges, was it our perception of the students or the students themselves that differed?

My conclusion, after studying and visiting schools in Great Britain, and researching in my own and others' classrooms in the United States, is that if we make the *learner* central to the process, instead of the *subject*, we change the outcome. One of my early research logs began with the following entry:

> I am really curious about the relationship of speaking and writing/thinking. Verbal proficiency seems to be linked, if not directly, to what we call intelligence, at least as measured through our testing, reasoning measurements. If all of language is interrelated—speak-

ing, writing, listening, and reading—and if the oral proficiency has a corresponding link to the written, then what things can we do—and do we do—in the classroom to enhance the spoken portion and then the written? I am particularly conscious of the need for students to speak in a variety of modes, to share experiences, to verbalize questions and concerns. Perhaps it is the classroom where elaborated responses can be made that will lead to more elaborated conceptions.

## Communication Is Basic

Speaking and listening are the motor and motivation for learning, and it is easy to see why. Communication is basic. From an infant's first cry, it is the voice that defines who we are as human beings. Our voice is our link to the outside world and our inner interpretation of that world. We shape our understandings by what we hear and how we relate those sounds and messages to our previous knowledge. Yes, we also communicate through reading and writing, but these acts are linked inextricably to the inner speech that fashions our thoughts and to the outer speech that refines them.

Of equal significance is the wider influence of the communication process. Each of us is constantly a sender and a receiver of messages. Every interaction creates new and often complex results—responses that in turn stimulate more effects. We communicate with our bodies, as well as with our voices. We send messages in the way we tilt our head, clear our throat, or fold a napkin. The process is complicated by the fact that the words we use to encode our ideas cannot be directly infused into the listener. The listener hears the message, decodes the words, interprets our body language, and constructs a meaning based on prior experiences and the current situation. A communication truism worth remembering is that meaning is in people, not in words. Communication is dynamic. It contains the power to transform a classroom into a rich, energy-filled environment when students, the traditional receivers, also become active senders. As such, they

3

*encode* messages instead of just *decoding* them. When that happens, the teacher's role changes as well. Now she must decode more actively in order for the exchange of ideas to grow in ever widening circles. Communication and learning are inseparable. As communication grows, so does learning. Evidence is accumulating that students who take an active role in constructing meaning, whether through inquiry, problem solving, or any number of methods that place them in the position of building knowledge, instead of just storing information, learn more and better.

## Communication and Learning

Even though communication is basic and dynamic, the oral part of learning is usually undervalued, unless it involves performance. Classroom talk is generally "transparent." It is used to get things done. This transparency and the transitory nature of talk contribute to our difficulty in regarding speech with as much seriousness as reading and writing. Yet it is by listening and speaking to others in ordinary conversation that we enlarge our experience background, not through simple addition, but through modification. Students naturally compare situations or people to their own experiences or television programs, as in this example from a twelfth grade class discussion of "The Rain Horse," by Ted Hughes:

STUDENT 1: Well, like if I go back to . . . like he imagined seeing this shape. This one crazy man . . . was on top of a hill looking down on a horse and turned around and tried to face the horse. So like he says it has to be something that takes more meaning than a horse. He's just laying on the hill and whether that is imaginary or real . . .
STUDENT 2: Has that ever happened to you? Do you think he sees something?
STUDENT 3: Yeah.
STUDENT 2: You've never pictured something that wasn't there? Like when you are in the house alone, then you hear something upstairs. You're downstairs watching a horror film and you hear

something upstairs, you know, and there is nothing there and you yell, "Who's there?"

Just as we do in ordinary conversations, these students assume other people's voices and attitudes, and by doing so "try on" new experiences. They build mock scenes and create hypothetical circumstances. As they discuss "The Rain Horse" they dramatize situations in an effort to better comprehend the meaning.

## Academic Achievement

Despite the lack of emphasis on talk in today's schools, prominent education theorists advocate that children should actively participate in the production of language, particularly speech, in order to learn more effectively (Britton 1970; Moffett 1968; Piaget and Inhelder 1966; Vygotsky 1979). Speech is connected to many aspects of learning. Fluent and proficient talk is demonstrably linked to writing and reading competencies (Loban 1976; Tough 1979). Abstract thought is enhanced when students have the chance for elaborated discourse, marked by the use of examples (Applebee 1978; Bernstein 1971). A highly developed vocabulary demonstrates a comparable conceptual growth (Bruner 1973). Cooperative learning enhances the intellect, since people inherently think better when they talk to others rather than when they work alone (Perkins 1992). Language versatility imbues students with self-confidence and inspires verbal risk taking. Conversely, when they lack words to encode thoughts, they are frustrated and their oral expression diminishes.

Not all scholars believe in a direct link between thought and speech. For instance, Michael Stubbs (1976), a sociolinguist, ascribes academic achievement to teacher expectation. He theorizes that verbal proficiency is perceived by teachers as a mark of superiority; therefore, they treat students differently who have this capability. Communication studies confirm that our society perceives verbally fluent individuals as possessing greater intelligence. Invariably, those who speak up in groups are given leadership roles.

But intelligence may be more than mere appearance for the verbally fluent child. We have evidence that children who talk, question, and actively discuss get higher scores and grades (Cornbleth 1976; Wittrock 1984). As the oral language-thought connection continues to be confirmed by new studies, David Perkins (1992), co-director of Harvard Project Zero—a research center for cognitive development—calls for a reorganization of schools to allow more cooperative learning.

## Knowledge Is Not Transmitted

The reason we need to talk to improve learning is that working with knowledge demands more than recall of information; it requires building knowledge structures. "Cognitive scientists today share with Piagetians a constructivist view of learning, asserting that people are not recorders of information but builders of knowledge structures" (Resnick and Klopfer 1989, 3). When we *know* something, it is not just information we have received. We must interpret the information and relate it to what we already know. If that is true, we cannot inoculate students with knowledge.

Even if most classrooms operate as if knowledge could be transmitted, it cannot. Cognitive research shows that meaningful knowledge must be generative. It should be used to solve problems and interpret new situations. In order to learn, students have to think through problems themselves. They have to create examples, question what they are told, and examine new data in relation to old. In fact, they have to build innovative knowledge structures. Talk achieves this generative knowledge, because as students plan, practice, and perform, they develop the dual skills of speech and thought (Parker and Goodkin 1987).

### The Social Nature of Thought

Speaking, by its nature, has a unique role in the development of the mind because it is a social act. We talk to others, whether it is one to many, as in public address, or one to one, as in interpersonal communication. The immediate feedback we receive from our audience heightens our perceptions and hastens our revisions more than does the delayed response we receive from written communication. Therefore the most important element in the thinking classroom, if students are to be meaning-makers, not just meaning-takers, is the social setting. Teachers must structure the process of learning along with the product, or knowledge. Resnick and Klopfer (1989) report that the most successful programs to promote higher-order cognition require students to solve problems and to design projects. And although these programs were initially conceived as individual work, experience showed that to achieve the best higher-order thinking, students had to interact socially.

Communication scholars will not be surprised by these findings. They have long understood the social nature of learning. For decades, they have known that oral communication affects all human behavior: our interactions with others, our reactions, and our thinking. These behaviors are directly related to the learning process. Speaking and listening, as well as reading and writing, affect the way we process information.

It is this rationale that prompts Charles Suhor (1988, 51) to advise language arts teachers of the need for oral communication. "To assure adequate process instruction in language, teachers at all levels should be encouraged, even mandated, to make extensive use of class discussion in large and small groups." Research in many fields supports the finding that classroom interaction improves learning. Students must have a variety of oral experiences: peer teaching, cooperative learning, and inquiry teaching.

Suhor admits that emphasizing discussion will have a profound impact on the image of schools as quiet places where children labor independently. Placing a value on discussion presupposes that "noisy" classrooms are a desirable outcome of English education instead of a sign of poor discipline. While English has distinct content, the goals of instruction are the *processing* of those materials through talking and writing. Eliciting language from students helps them to shape meaning from experience, their own as well as those imaginary worlds on the printed page. We see this process in action in another small group discussion of "The Rain Horse," by Ted Hughes. The students try to visualize the setting and relate the character's actions to their own experiences. They even practice using the character's voice as a motivation test.

VEETA: What kind of place is this we are in?

MAUREEN: It's a farm or something. Isn't he on his farm—like where he used to live? And didn't he say that he hadn't been there for twelve years and this was an unknown land or something?

VEETA: Okay, why was he walking in the rain?

MAUREEN: That's what I didn't see especially.

KATHY: I think he was probably walking before it started to rain. I mean he didn't say, "Oh, it's raining. I'm going outside. Looks like a thunderstorm! I'll put on my best suit and hike up the mountain!"

CARRIE: Okay, why is he angry?

KATHY: Who's angry?

CARRIE: The guy.

MAUREEN: Because this horse is chasing him and he is in the rain and he is going to ruin his suit.

KATHY: I think he is having mental torment. I mean, I think there is something else bothering him than just the fact that it is raining, you know. I think he was really mad and that's why he went for a walk to begin with. You know, like sometimes, you are just—Agh!

An important goal for language arts, in addition to helping children meet basic competencies, is letting them discover that learning is fun. The social part of learning creates the pleasure. Suhor does not say this, nor do other researchers, but fun is the fuel that makes learning a light and easy burden. It is also a way to cultivate a nation of lifetime learners.

## Functions of Language

Developing language orally is a way to develop thinking. It is not the only way, but it is a necessary and key way. By giving students power over language, we enable them to have power over their thought processes. If language is the means by which we gain control over our thinking, and speech is the primary mode for the process, we need to look at speech to see how it uniquely performs this function.

## Expressive Speech

Our language changes as the function changes. It ranges from transactional in the participant role to poetic in the spectator role, to use James Britton's (1982) terms. As we cross the barrier between the two roles we use expressive speech, loosely structured and self-revealing. This type of speech is flexible, marked by tentativeness and use of filler words or sounds such as "you know" or "um." Expressive speech, because of its lack of fluency and its syntactic errors, is often viewed negatively, even though it is the most valuable form of language in the classroom.

Therefore, teachers must encourage expressive speech. If language is the business of the classroom, the environment should be one where learners can experiment with all forms of speech—the transactional and poetic, but especially the expressive. Talking and listening must be treated with as much respect as reading and writing, since they are the media through which learning takes place.

## Attributes Linking Speech to Thought

We can identify at least seven attributes of oral communication that relate directly to the control of thought processes.

1. Outer speech is for an *audience*. An audience demands clarity. The less informed the audience, the more the speaker has to explain.
2. *Expressive* speech is higher in hypotheses and testing devices. It is marked by tentativeness and questioning, and it is more open to modification than statements presented in perfect or elaborate forms.

9

3. Speech is *reflexive*. Through talk we receive meaningful perceptions of others' worlds. From these data, we can reinterpret their experiences and adapt them to our own.

4. *Rearticulation* of ideas establishes concepts. Rehearsing aloud, putting a process into words, and repeating the process in response to questions improve learning performance.

5. Speech enhances *decentration*, a necessary condition for abstract thought. Speech helps us to stand outside our own knowledge. As a spectator, we can incorporate others' viewpoints into our own inner views.

6. Discourse improves *thought elaboration*. Sharing thoughts in a discussion creates an enriched pool of information. The combined effort affords a unique progression of ideas, not possible for any single individual.

7. *Interpersonal* speech becomes *intrapersonal*. The process of group hypothesizing, testing, and questioning is transferred to individual thought patterns (Barnes 1976).

The following transcript of a small group discussing the short story "The Witness" by Doris Lessing demonstrates several of these attributes:

VEETA: What kind of characteristics does Miss Ives have?

KATHY: She is rude?

MAUREEN: Was she an old maid? She wasn't married, was she?

KATHY: She isn't old and I think she liked Mr. Brooke, but she was afraid to because no one else did.

VEETA: Yeah.

MAUREEN: They both hated Marnie. Miss Ives and Miss Jenkins both hated Marnie and they were probably both threatened by her because she was so young and vivacious. They were just boring old maids.

CARRIE: And they didn't have the boss coming up to them and saying, "You're going to get married."

KATHY: What was the deal with the secretaries?

VEETA: I want to know what kind of business it was.

MAUREEN: They had about five typists and an accountant.

CARRIE: And two old ladies and a do-nothing,

MAUREEN: I didn't like the—

CARRIE: The boss, Mr. Jones.

MAUREEN: Why didn't they get married?

KATHY: They were having an affair!

MAUREEN: He and Marnie?

KATHY: Yeah. Didn't you understand that when you read it?

MAUREEN: But she's a friend's daughter!

KATHY: But so what? Hey? [Reading] "There were Marnie and Mr. Jones. His face buried in her hair, and he was saying, 'Please, Marnie, please, please, please . . .' Mr. Brooke stared, his eyes focusing with difficulty. Then Marnie gave a little scream and Mr. Jones jumped up and came across. 'Spying!' he said angrily." I mean what could he have been spying on if there's just a friend's daughter and they're just, you know.

MAUREEN: I thought maybe he was, like, trying to molest her.

KATHY: Uh huh. But she was kind of enjoying this. Why would he keep her around the office when she kept saying she wanted to go home. But, no, he said she couldn't go home and stuff like that.

MAUREEN: Yeah.

KATHY: I think Miss Ives is so vicious, vindictive. She's trying to get everybody back for everything anybody's ever done to her in her lifetime. She just seems to be reaching out for someone, too. I don't see why her and Mr. Brooke don't get it together.

The above discussion illustrates how oral communication is linked to thought. It is marked by various hypotheses. Miss Ives liked Mr. Brooke. Miss Ives and Miss Jenkins were threatened by Marnie's youth, and Marnie's relationship to Mr. Jones is explained in different ways. The discussion also has a tentative and questioning tone that invites response. Differing views of the characters and situations emerge and are tested against the "evidence," the text. Decentration, or the movement away from egocentric thought, occurs as the speakers try to envision the relationships between the characters and their possible emotions. Veeta's question about the characteristics of Miss Ives becomes elaborated even though the conversation travels to other people and incidents in a seemingly random pattern. This kind of expressive speech is more likely to occur in child-peer conversations than in child-teacher conversations.

## Form of Discourse

The above transcript illustrates an important characteristic of expressive speech. Note the prevalence of the filler word "like." Traditional speech instruction would eliminate such vocal additions as "like" and "you know." In public address, one speaker to many, we are taught these words weaken the message and should be avoided. They indicate the speaker's tentativeness. A public speaker using superfluous words loses credibility. However, in natural conversation we need filler words to provide the "space" for us to gather our thoughts. If we look at the transcript, "like" precedes new thoughts. An additional benefit of this pattern is that it sends a signal that others can join in and take risks with their ideas, as well. If speakers in a seminar or small group discussion make definitive statements, using no filler words and no questions, they limit an open interchange of ideas. We are hesitant to challenge experts.

## *Speech and Education*

We can say that communication is the essence of teaching. "The teacher and student are linked in a *system* of simultaneous communication transactions" (Cooper 1995, 7). And much of what happens in communication may occur without explicit awareness, good or bad. By raising awareness of the communication system, we can improve the quality of communication for all participants, the teacher as well as the students.

Although research and experience demonstrate the value of discussion, whether teacher directed, large group, or small group, the opportunities for students to experience this style of learning are extremely limited. For example, a survey of one twelfth grade class, about their participation, attitudes, and opportunity for discussion in subject-area classes revealed minimal involvement. Only 50 percent of the students described themselves as frequent participants in classroom discussions. They reported discussions were held in approximately two classes a day. While the number of students is small in this survey, it reflects the general findings of researchers (O'Keefe 1988b).

Meaningful thinking is necessary for the individual. It is also essential for our civilization. A democratic society depends on the voices of the people. There is a social purpose in public education. Thomas Jefferson, the father of American public schooling, believed that democracy could not survive without an educated people making informed choices. Rhetoric, or the study of the spoken word, was a required subject in our early history and only disappeared in this century, with current language arts education emphasizing writing instead of speech. The change in emphasis is reflected in teacher preparation.

## Inadequate Instruction

Speech instruction has disappeared from many teacher educational programs, in spite of the fact that teachers spend the greater part of their day as "public speakers." Of the states that require the National Teacher Examination, speech teachers are the only ones tested for knowledge of communication (McCaleb 1989).

Stranger still is the lack of attention to speaking and listening in the K–12 classroom, given our increasingly diverse population. Many students enter our schools today speaking English as a second language. Facility with spoken English speeds their learning to read and write. Other groups of students have strong oral traditions. These children could enjoy success with spoken language. At the same time they would learn valuable ways to organize their ideas in writing because oral language fluency translates into written language fluency. Speaking builds both thinking and writing strengths. It also positively influences reading comprehension (Wittrock 1984).

Nevertheless, speaking and listening training is largely absent in schools. Most students receive little formal training in oral communication skills. The fact that children know "how to talk" creates an impression that limited resources should not be spent on speech communication instruction. Only two states demand completion of a public speaking course as a requirement for high school graduation (*Guidelines* 1991). The other forty-eight states do not require any type of oral communication course. Therefore the only exposure students have to speech is through their language arts teachers. Communication instruction should be incorporated across the curriculum, but it has to start in English classes. Unfortunately, language arts teachers have not studied oral communication, any more than have mathematics or science teachers, unless they chose to specialize in theatre or public speaking as well as English. Ironically, the responsibility for increasing speech skills lies on those who have primarily studied literature and composition.

Student textbooks offer little help in solving this dilemma. A sharp division exists between English and Speech textbooks. The former offer hints to include talk as part of an integrated language arts program with such instructions as: "Discuss the idea of . . ." But no guidance helps the teacher to set up a real discussion. Conversely, current speech textbooks, while giving detailed information about improving speaking and listening skills in discussion and public address, pay no attention to the integration of speaking and listening with the other language acts of writing and reading (O'Keefe 1992). Expertise from both kinds of professionals should be combined for the enrichment of instruction.

## Talk Is Essential

All of the challenges schools face now (violence, drugs, teen pregnancy, poverty, illiteracy, ethnic and racial tension) will be here tomorrow, as will increasing pressure for an education to meet global competition. While public schools cannot eradicate the problems of our society, they can help to educate our students to cope with them. No longer can we believe that ability counts more than effort. For instance, an elitist attitude toward rhetoric and sophisticated thought, providing speaking opportunities and training only for leaders, for advanced placement and honor students, has no place in our schools today. All children, regardless of ability level, must have speaking and listening instruction as part of their basic education. Talk is as essential to thought as exercise is to health. This book is designed to show how a language arts classroom, without sacrificing content, can meet those aims.

*Teacher-Researcher Questions*
1. How might small groups help students to generate ideas in prewriting sessions?
2. How do understandings change as students engage in creative speaking activities related to a text?
3. What changes in attitudes toward literature occur when students prepare and deliver oral readings? *They have to get into the "head" of the*
4. What kinds of oral interpretations of a text contribute posi- *character,* tively to reading comprehension? *speak as they do (formally) sometimes*

*→ Students could not be seeing an imp. point, fact, + orally, he*

## • ACTIVITIES •

TWENTY SPEECH ACTIVITIES *can be made* TO USE IN AN ENGLISH CLASS *aware of this (class discussion)*

---

OBJECTIVE: Students become actively involved in making meaning through speaking and listening when those experiences occur frequently in the instructional program.

PROCESS: These suggestions can be implemented throughout the school year. More detailed information on setting up groups, asking questions, overcoming shyness, and evaluating are included in other chapters of this book. *look at this*

1. Students can give prepared, short (three-minute) daily readings at the beginning of the class period from books

they have particularly enjoyed. These may follow a theme. Similarly, students can read original works.

2. A local author can visit the class to give readings and/or talk about his or her writing.

3. Students can tape a "Book Program" in which a group discusses one book or members contribute short reviews of different titles.

4. Students can retell a short extract from a story as a radio play on tape (with sound effects, introductory music, etc.). The tape can be played back to the class or to other classes. This idea can be used with original scripts as well.

5. A sound and light show can be made to illustrate poetry, original or published, using taped music, projected pictures, and live or taped readings.

6. Groups can be assigned to "sell" a book to readers of their own age. The group pretends it has been hired by a publisher to promote the book. This can be spoken, audiotaped, or videotaped.

7. A simulated phone-in program can be conducted with calls either to characters in a book, asking about their motives, attitudes, etc., or to the author.

8. Students can pair off to study a character in a play. Then they can be interviewed by the class as if one were the character, the other the biographer.

9. A group acts out a scenario as if they were employed by a movie tycoon who is considering making their book into a script. Would the book make a good film? Why? Who would go see it? Why? Does the dialogue sound real? What stars would play the roles?

10. Pupils can work in pairs in which one plays a journalist, the other, the author. The journalist questions the author about plot, characters, setting, and the way the book is written.

11. Students can conduct a *post mortem*, in which members of the class discuss in role as characters in a novel the parts they have played. This activity fosters close examination of motivation. For example, a character who has been a

16

victim in the plot may challenge the actions of more powerful characters. Discussion should be consistent with the text.

12. A variation of the above can be held. One character (perhaps represented by several students), placed on a witness stand for cross-examination, answers questions posed by lawyers representing another character or the class community.

13. The teacher can read aloud important passages of a book to impart the enjoyment and entertainment aspect of reading literature.

14. Pupils in twos or threes can read aloud to each other parts of a book the class is studying.

15. A guest can read portions of a book to the class. This guest could be a parent, a school staff member, an older student or sibling—anyone who loves to read and does so well.

16. Tapes can be played of readings by unknown or professional readers.

17. Students can retell a story they have recently read by means of a game. Teams of students plan Jeopardy-like questions about elements of the plot or character behaviors. They take turns with their quizzing of classmates. This works especially well with more involved novels— e.g., *A Tale of Two Cities.*

18. A group or class can role-play an improvisation of a scene from a novel or short story.

19. In a variation on the foregoing, students can role-play the same characters at some point in time (maybe years) before a particular situation in a novel or short story occurs.

20. The teacher can role-play the author while the class is in the process of reading a book. The class asks questions for clarification and makes comments about the book so far. The "author" does not tell them what is going to happen.

WHY THIS WORKS: Students define what they know as they become responsible for interpreting information. They learn to value speaking and listening as part of the process of instruction and learn that visibility improves the skills of communication and strengthens its legitimate place in more effective learning.

## DISCUSSION IDEAS

OBJECTIVE: The goal of this activity is to increase the students' participation in discussion. They learn to listen for main ideas and practice forming questions to probe for meanings.
PROCESS:

1. Appoint two people as note takers, recorders during a lecture or a film. Ask them to read those portions of the notes that they feel were the most significant. Ask other students to add in other information they remembered. Discuss why these ideas were most important.

2. Assign all students the task of writing down three questions while listening to a lecture or viewing a film. After the lecture, form a large circle. Students take turns asking their questions of the class. Class members assume the primary responsibility for answering the questions, not the teacher. A recorder keeps track of the questions, answers, and provides a summary. Unanswered questions can become part of the homework for the next day's lesson.

WHY THIS WORKS: Students assume responsibility and ownership for the process of learning. Competence and confidence in this role improves performance.

## SOCIAL ISSUES

OBJECTIVE: Students develop an appreciation for the underlying meaning in a work of literature beyond its plot structure.
PROCESS:

1. Brainstorm for possible social issues related to a literary text the class is studying.

Example: In *Wuthering Heights,* by Emily Brontë, relevant social issues include class and racial prejudice, child and spouse abuse, alcoholism, women's rights, inheritance laws.

2. Students read about and research those issues in today's society.
3. Each student or group presents findings on a particular social issue.
4. Each student or group in charge of a particular issue compiles a list of examples and observations from the text that relate to the social issue.
5. With the teacher-moderator, or a student-moderator, the class discusses the issue as it relates to the novel.
6. Follow up with a writing assignment. Students write an informal journal piece about how the text relates to the social issue. What understandings has the student gained about the issue through the text? Attached to that writing can be the research and text notes about the particular issue.

WHY THIS WORKS: This activity relates a text to the real world. Students can find a "way into" a text through contemporary issues. This is the kind of discussion that allows everyone to speak and offer opinions, whether about the issue or the text.

## PREWRITING BRAINSTORMING

OBJECTIVE: Students assist each other in generating ideas in order to prepare a longer written piece.
PROCESS:

1. Prepare a worksheet for each student with specific directions on the topic to be discussed. For example:
   a. Describe the setting of the novel. What features of this setting contribute to the mood, the conflict, the character development? In what ways does the setting uniquely contribute to the plot or the meaning of the work?

b. Select a main character. What are the main traits of this character? How do these traits contribute to the development of plot or theme? How do these traits contribute to the reader's involvement?

2. Divide students into small groups. Each group brainstorms ideas, and students take notes on their own worksheets.

3. After brainstorming about these or similar questions, students take their discussion notes and write individual essays. Although the group has generated ideas collaboratively, each individual composes an essay that reflects his or her own choices.

4. The students meet again in these same groups to share their essays as the first step in revision. Another method could be to write a collaborative essay.

WHY THIS WORKS: Students enjoy sharing ideas in a nonthreatening setting. Finding out what others think about the topic helps to unlock ideas, bridging the hurdle of "how to begin" writing or "what do I say?" problems.

# ● *Two*

. . . . . . . . . . . . . . . .

## *Teaching for Discovery*

Children enter school as question marks and leave as
periods.                                     *—Postman and Weingartner*

We visit a ninth grade classroom where the students
are meeting in small groups discussing *To Kill a Mockingbird*,
by Harper Lee. Their task is to share their original questions
about the text and to select two from their combined list for a
discussion with the whole class. We listen as a group tackles
the questions of one of its members.

STUDENT A: Do you think it was wrong for the sheriff to protect
the truth in this—[Boo's killing of Mr. Ewell]?
STUDENT B: No matter what, it is always wrong to protect some-
body—who killed somebody.
STUDENT C: I think it wasn't wrong because, I mean, Boo did
something good, and he has been entitled to protect his kids from
death—so—
STUDENT D: I don't think it's wrong that he did it, but I think it
is kind of wrong that, I mean, that they tried to cover it up.
STUDENT C: I mean, he did it for the kids—so—
STUDENT E: I don't think it was wrong—
STUDENT A: The murder?
STUDENT E: Yeah, the murder, because it was self-defense, even
if the jury might not believe that, and he was just protecting them.
STUDENT C: I think it was right to cover up because it was self-
defense. He was just trying to help.

What we have been observing is a group of students trying
to discover meaning. The information has been read (the text

*21*

of *To Kill a Mockingbird*), but obviously the rightness or wrongness of the characters' actions is problematical. The meaning behind the "facts" is also part of the knowledge. Discovering that meaning is a cooperative process.

## Instructional Modes

We must look carefully at the process of learning and find its relationship to the subject's content. Since we always think about *something*, the knowledge of the classroom is undeniably important. *How* students acquire that information, or the process of constructing knowledge, is equally important. We can basically divide the teaching process into two instructional modes: the transmission of knowledge or the discovery of knowledge. In the transmission mode the students are cast in the role of learner-answerer; in the discovery mode, they are learner-questioners.

### The Transmission Mode

Traditionally, the transmission mode, sometimes called the expository mode, is the more common form of instruction. The teacher decides the pace, content, and manipulation of material, dominating the communication acts of the classroom. Students primarily listen; teachers primarily speak. This communication pattern is well established. Instruction sometimes requires transmission. The problem is that when it is overused or the sole instructional method, it has damaging results.

#### Pseudoquestions

Students expect a recurring sequence of teacher questions for which the teacher has a preexisting answer in mind. "Known-answer" or "pseudo" questions signal the teacher's authority. Thus, while teacher-made questions are supposed to build knowledge, they often limit students' opportunities to learn because they primarily target recall of information. These questions, overemphasizing recall or acquisition of information, leave minimal time for comprehension or reasoning tasks.

## *Limited Student Response*

In an effort to cover a course's content, teachers have to limit the number and kinds of student responses. Sad to say, researchers have found that low achievers asked as many questions as the other children when they were in kindergarten, but by upper elementary and secondary classes, low achievers asked significantly fewer questions than did their peers (Good and Brophy 1991). This behavior suggests that the need to cover material causes teachers to squelch or limit low achievers' questions and responses in favor of keeping the pace of a lesson flowing.

## *Learned Passivity*

Since low achievers are less likely to answer correctly, and since their mistakes are on public view, they face considerably more risk when they participate actively. A good strategy is for them to remain passive. They can avoid being called upon by using nonverbal methods such as not looking at the teacher or just shaking their heads. These behaviors, they have learned, diminish the chance of having to interact publicly.

But low achievers are not the only ones who have learned to withdraw. Developed passivity in the transmission mode classroom is pervasive. Douglas Barnes, a British researcher, transcribed communication in secondary classes for several weeks. What surprised him most was student passivity. "They asked no questions and made no suggestions. It was as if they had no curiosity" (1990 p. 45). When he studied the transcripts, however, the reason became apparent. The teachers did not ask the students to contribute ideas from their own experience. The pupils asked questions to confirm only that they had grasped the teacher's messages.

[The students] played no active role in their learning, they made no attempt to test whether they had understood, to raise contrary examples, or to make links with their out-of-school experience. (p. 45)

Just one or two teachers tried to elicit responses from students about their ideas or their understanding of the lesson. Yet this kind of feedback is an essential part of both the communication process and the process of building meaning.

Teachers have learned effectively to *prevent* classroom talk. Negative methods to control discourse include sarcasm and ridicule. In the best classes the transmission format precludes original student input. In the worst classes, denigrating devices keep students quiet.

## The Discovery Mode

The structure of the transmission pattern, however familiar and convenient, is not optimum if we want students to authentically learn. Students need to be questioners, seekers of information. The impetus for discovery is the impetus for learning. Motivation to learn increases when the task is an adventure, when the act of discovery forces students to make connections and thereby construct new meanings. Nevertheless, Bob, a graduate education student, expresses realistic concerns about the problems of discovery mode instruction:

> For example, if a teacher views his or her priority task as imparting information to students, it is not likely that he or she will allocate the time required for students to analyze and discover for themselves critical relationships among the subject matter or to develop their own theses that challenge those presented to them. An obsession with coverage of the subject is an enemy to developing critical thinking skills in students. Student-centered activities entail an element of risk in that the instructor gives up the monopoly on the ordering of ideas and rather than directing must influence or guide the discussion. Control beyond guidance or influence will stifle the ownership that students take in the discussion in all but the most mature groups. . . . It is a tough and demanding regime for teachers and one that requires greater, not lesser, preparation than teacher-centered methods.

In the discovery mode it must be the students who question, not just the teachers, and the questions must be real, not teacher-made pseudoquestions. The more students approach learning as a task of discovering, the more they are truly motivated to learn. For example, students can learn to improve their reading better when they want to unlock the meaning of an interesting story rather than when they are confronted with drill and skill exercises. Discovery places the teacher and the students in a cooperative position as they decide speech acts. As children make decisions about when and what to question, and when and what to answer, they gain the power to generate additional ideas. They begin to understand that mistakes or misunderstandings are not to be confused with success or failure. Learning becomes a form of hypothesis testing, the process of forming and testing theories, much as scientists do. During hypothesis testing, the goal is often changed as new information reveals a different angle on a problem.

Critical thinking requires the ability to ask questions that penetrate a topic and reveal its complexity. If we allow students' questions to guide instruction, we utilize both a process and a product. Students search out information and also learn how to ask good questions.

For example, we can study a transcript of the same ninth grade class mentioned earlier, as one of the groups leads the whole class discussion with their chosen question. Discourse moves from factual/recall responses to metaphorical interpretations:

STUDENT LEADER: Why does Boo Radley feel comfortable in the dark?

STUDENT A: He's not accepted. He stayed in the house, in the dark, in the basement. Maybe he was shy. All the bad stuff that happened.

STUDENT B: He's never been anywhere besides the dark. He's always in the dark.

STUDENT C: He doesn't know how to deal with the light. He was kept in the dark.

STUDENT D: He couldn't see himself. Ghosts come out in the dark. He's Boo.
STUDENT E: He's sensitive to light.
STUDENT F: The dark is a friend. He's comfortable in the dark. Afraid of the light.

Contrast that dialogue to one about "Dandelions" by Deborah Austin in a transmission class:

TEACHER: What experience does the poem describe?
STUDENT: War.
TEACHER: Good.

After the class, this observer asked the student how the experience of war fit with the title. The student said, "I didn't know it was about dandelions."

### The Role of Questioning

For all of us, teachers and students alike, questioning is a fundamental way to improve our thinking. Frank Smith (1990, 129) observes:

> The first thing to be done to improve the quality of thinking in all educational institutions, from grade school to graduate school, is perhaps the most radical. Students—and teachers—must learn to doubt.

The fear of facing challenges to our deeply held beliefs may inhibit our own questioning. We do not welcome the uncertainty of not knowing the answers, and we do not press for students' inquiries that may disturb our convictions. But these are the very fears we must overcome. As teachers for thinking we have to surmount our acceptance of time-honored methods and assumptions. Nor should we hesitate to doubt others' ideas. Facts can masquerade as opinions and vice versa, no matter how dearly they are held.

Critical thinking *begins* when we realize the need to rethink and reevaluate the way things are. It considers all alternatives and resists formulaic methods for making decisions. It is when we are certain that what *was* so is *still* so that our growth as thinkers stops. For that reason, real questioning should flourish in our classrooms. Students and teachers must accept the questioning and probing stance of investigators. As a community of learners, we must look for better understanding of reality and its attendant implications. Leaving the transmission mode, at least part of the time, improves instruction without destroying control. Discovery can be channeled, without being forced. Letting go is not the same as giving up.

### Questioning and Critical Thinking

When students become questioners they discover their own ideas. They have the chance to explore, argue, and sharpen critical thinking skills. Student questions give teachers valuable information about their progress and possible misunderstandings. When they are asked to generate questions in response to literature texts, they often reveal the need for factual information that the teacher assumes they know. Here are examples of such student questions:

> From a twelfth grade regular class studying *The Heart of the Matter*, by Graham Greene: Who are Father Rank's children? [Father Rank is a priest.] What war is taking place?
> From a twelfth grade regular class studying *Wuthering Heights:* Are there two Catherines? Is Joseph black?
> From a ninth grade regular class studying *To Kill a Mockingbird:* Why does Boo Radley eat squirrels and cats? Are Jem and Scout black?

Although an important advantage for student questioning is feedback to the teacher, the key goal is for students to learn what *they* know, test what *they* know, and revise what *they* know. By asking questions they take the hardest step, since recognizing a problem is the only way to begin to solve it. Unfortunately, finding problems is the phase of teaching that is still most neglected. As Frank Smith (1990, 129) tells us, "All thinking is based on 'suppose things were different.' Critical thinking begins with readiness to challenge received wisdom."

One reason teachers resist the discovery mode and student questioning is that they fear student questions will not be challenging enough. Marzano (1992) provides anecdotal evidence of teachers who used student-created questions successfully. He reports their surprise when they found that the questions students asked far surpassed the level of difficulty they would have expected. Students are capable of developing probing questions that can generate in-depth discussions. The following list is a sampling of one compiled in twenty minutes by twelfth grade students after reading *Wuthering Heights*.

Why isn't Hareton more developed as a character?

What is the role of Mr. Lockwood? Is it more than a means to get a story from Mrs. Dean?

Is Heathcliff influenced more by heredity or environment?

How does Heathcliff's origin and past affect the story?

Is it out of character for Heathcliff to let himself die? If all he wanted was to be with Catherine, why didn't he die sooner?

Why did Isabella marry Heathcliff, knowing he was obsessed with Catherine?

Why is Edgar so naive about Catherine's obvious attraction to Heathcliff?

Why did Catherine love Heathcliff?

## Learner Attitudes

Unfortunately, no matter how excellent a teacher's methods may be, the students' ability to learn is controlled by their attitudes as well as their aptitudes. For good learning (and good questioning) to take place, the learner must be willing to engage mentally. Three factors can have a negative influence on students' active participation: learned helplessness, focus of control, and self-concept.

### Learned Helplessness

The term "learned helplessness" refers to the theory that when children's expectations for behavior consequences are not consistently reinforced, they may react by doing nothing. When learned helplessness interferes with communication, children withdraw. Those who are ignored one day and receive an overabundance of attention another may react by becoming passive. Children, for example, may say something at home and be praised, then say that same thing at school and be greeted with ridicule or disapproval. Or a child may be encouraged to talk by one parent and punished for doing so by the other. Helplessness, then, may result in communication withdrawal (McCroskey and Richmond 1991).

## Focus of Control

Another problem is that students perceive that the control of communication is the teacher's responsibility. Most commonly they ask the teacher to elaborate, repeat the message, or give an example. Yet if the focus of control had been on the students as listeners, it is likely they would have taken some responsibility for clarification, attempting to supply an example or test for understanding.

In large classes, students may abandon clarification strategies altogether and simply ignore the problem. Interesting to note, most studies look at questioning responses solely as an effort to clarify teacher messages, placing the focus of control on the teacher. Student behavior is not surprising when we recognize that the transmission mode promotes this kind of dependency.

## Self-Concept

All children develop a self-concept about their role in the classroom through their communication experiences. Low achievers suffer from low self-concepts when their efforts are ignored or undervalued. They often have fewer opportunities to shine publicly. They may not be asked to do such exciting things as making up stories aloud, creating riddles, or dramatizing parts. Their tasks tend to be the repetitive stuff of worksheets and drills. Thus they have less choice of assignments and correspondingly less autonomy and responsibility. Gifted and average, as well as low achievers, have concerns about teacher approval and peer acceptance, especially when they reach adolescence.

Maureen and Carrie, twelfth grade students, reflect this worry about their participation in another class, although they had been leading group discussions in English.

MAUREEN: I am still afraid to speak in my Government class because there are people in there that will contradict you, you know, just to contradict you.

CARRIE: "It's nice out today." "No, it's kind of cloudy."

MAUREEN: Just to make you angry—they are just out there to make your life miserable. I mean they are just there to irritate you and try to make you uncomfortable in the classroom.

Kathy offers advice about involving passive students in classroom communication.

*Student insight*

KATHY: Make them feel like they have to do something. Make them feel like it is important that they participate. Because they will probably just sit there and think, like—"They don't care what I say anyway. I'm just here—there are thirty other people in the class so let them talk. What I have to say isn't important."

What anybody has to say is important. I mean it could be a totally new idea, a new perspective and something that someone doesn't understand. That person may just be sitting there with a mind full of knowledge.

*Key pt.*

Students must perceive themselves as worthy of recognition. They must know that their ideas are valued and that their contributions are essential for the group.

## Overcoming the Barriers

When learning is viewed as a cooperative venture between teacher and students, then students must assume a more active role in the communication and learning process. Since students take their cues from teachers' behaviors, the teacher must first convey her shift to a discovery mode. Through her own actions, the teacher demonstrates the value of reflection over rightness and the value of questions over answers. Unfortunately, some teachers seem unable to take this step. They devalue student opinions and cut off free exchange, perhaps unconsciously. The twelfth graders describe the kind of classroom environments that help or hinder talk.

MAUREEN: I think making the students feel comfortable and at ease and letting them know that you are there for their benefit and letting them know that you do care . . . and when the students are comfortable and they like the teacher or the teacher likes them, they want to learn. They want to broaden their horizons.

CARRIE: Yeah, because some teachers if you say something, they will laugh at you—

TINA: [Mentioning a teacher]—if you try to get into a discussion and you say something that he doesn't agree with, he will laugh at you or crack a joke about it and make you feel—like—stupid.

Students will not generate their own questions in an atmosphere where the act of asking a question is interpreted as a failure to understand or even to pay attention. Obviously, they must be in an environment where they feel the exchange of ideas is a healthy, nonthreatening one. They must feel the strength of their own self-concept as a capable learner.

Students who have positive self-concepts about their ability sense that the focus of control is within themselves and are not subject to learned helplessness. They maintain independence in the learning situation and can become active discoverers when required. A ninth grade gifted English class discussion illustrates this kind of self-initiation as the students examine *A Tale of Two Cities*.

STUDENT A: Why is Gaspard under the carriage?
STUDENT B: Where does it say Gaspard is the murderer?
TEACHER: You're right, it doesn't say.
STUDENT C: I got mixed up.
STUDENT D: He was a stowaway?
STUDENT E: I didn't know how it connected.
STUDENT F: Will it become clearer?
STUDENT G: Is there a line that says that?

No passivity is evident here. Through this line of questioning and response the students, as well as the teacher, sort out

Dickens' indirect prose. They learn that Gaspard had hidden under the carriage and was, indeed, Monsieur the Marquis' murderer.

## *Questioning and Intelligence*

The ability to question well appears to depend upon both cognitive and communication skills. Therefore, enhancing the ability to question has the possibility of improving competence in both areas. In at least one study to determine if intelligence and questioning were related, no significant difference was noted between subjects who were highly complex cognitively—that is, able to form more involved impressions of people and events—and those who were not (Rubin and Henzl 1984). Subjects were also equally able to distinguish fact from opinion, identify main ideas, summarize, and defend a point of view. One conclusion of this research is that training individuals to question and to engage in more complex communication acts could positively affect cognitive abilities. In other words, instead of cognitive strength preceding communication, the reverse may be true.

There is a plausible explanation for this connection. Increasing the opportunity and complexity of communication experiences encourages students to create a repertoire of responses. Developing that repertoire might in turn work to increase cognitive complexity. It is possible that neural networks become more complex as individuals are challenged by more complex situations. As students question and challenge conclusions, premises, and opinions to probe for meanings, their capacity for complex thought will likely expand. When students interact with their peers in discovery activities, they learn about the topic, but they also learn diverse ways to communicate.

## *Pedagogical Concerns*

Once we decide to change the climate, deciding where and how to intervene poses some problems. Expert learners, apparently, have spontaneously developed their own repertoire of cognitive and metacognitive strategies, enabling them to effectively attack learning problems. If we force a skill-based instructional approach on them it might impede their natural capabilities. On the other hand, these same learners may encounter difficulties in new situations when old methods no longer work. This kind of student can profit from more awareness of his or her natural strategies.

Less proficient students can advance both their communication and thinking skills when the instruction is devised to support these functions. How much intervention is needed and when to use it becomes a situational decision for the teacher.

Since younger students or less proficient ones tend to view their learning as accidental, they take a less active part in the planning and structuring of their work (Jones, Pallincsar, Ogle, and Carr 1987). Learning when and how to question could place a very effective strategy in the hands of these students.

## Questioning Competency

It would seem that school administrators and pedagogical pattern-setters have often implicitly decided that students are not qualified to ask academic questions. Recommended teacher time-management strategies and questioning tactics virtually preclude student opportunity for questioning. Numerous programs for improving learning outcomes have been marketed focusing on teacher behaviors: Teacher Effectiveness and Student Achievement (TESA), Skillful Teacher, and the Jane Stallings and Madeline Hunter methods. These behavioristic programs often assume that when students question, it is an indication of noncomprehension. Something went wrong with the instruction.

As a participant in a project to improve minority achievement in my secondary school, I was trained in the "Effective Use of Time Program" developed by the Peabody Center for Effective Teaching at Vanderbilt University. The coding is intensive and remarkably accurate, but there are flaws in the system. No allowance is made for students speaking in a meaningful manner without the teacher, nor for writing-to-learn activities. Both activities create negative scores. This program assumes that if students are talking, they are wasting time. If they are writing, it is busy work. In fact, "students initiating remarks" is considered equal to "shout-outs," and carries the same negative connotations as that term in any teacher's evaluation.

The results of the observations of my class showed that despite students asking questions four times as often as the program desired, 84 percent of the class' statements were about academic content—an exceedingly high percentage compared to national averages. Students talked and questioned, yet maintained academic time-on-task—which has been positively associated with higher achievement and better learning.

## Questioning in Small Groups

I was interested in a comparison between student questioning and talk in small group versus whole class discussions. For that reason, I looked at the interactions of the same class as part of my own study. While the percentage of time that students asked questions in the whole class discussion was not much different from the sessions observed by outsiders, when the same students were in small groups they asked significantly more questions.

During two small group discussions, although no teacher was present, almost one-fourth of the comments were academic questions. I included as academic questions those that related the text to personal experiences as well as those more directly connected to the content. Examples are:

What would you do if no one loved you?
Why was he so rude?
Why did they keep him around if he was such a jerk?

Of course, all of the comments during small group discussion are by necessity self-initiated. This demand for self-initiation may be the strongest argument for including small group work as a classroom method.

The smaller number is not the only reason for more participation; students are more likely to know and trust the other participants. Maureen, one of the students, makes this observation:

> I think that people are more at ease with what they are saying in a smaller group, especially if you are among friends. You don't mind saying what you really feel. They'll understand what you are saying.

Small groups are valuable, but should not take the place of whole class discussion. Kathy, another one of the students, speaks of the advantages of both forms of discussion:

> In small groups you learn more, but in the large groups you get everybody talking and you get a wider range of points of view.

## *Students as Questioners*

Allowing students time to build questions is not the whole answer. The lesson design must provide a structure for questioning. We have to help children to ask hard questions, ones that challenge assumptions, probe underlying causes, and find contradictions. Students have to learn to examine their world views and their attitudes.

The questioning class is a dynamic one. While control is not abandoned, it is changed. Students learn to accept responsibility for building their own knowledge. The difficult task of finding and asking questions is shared in a nonthreatening environment. Teachers become listeners. Students become questioners. The percentages for students' talk-time increases profitably, especially the percentage of self-initiated comments—the kind of talk that indicates kids are thinking. We do not have to jettison content, nor should we apply questioning as a sort of decorative frosting on the serious business of the classroom. We must reevaluate our regular work and change the way we go about it.

*Teacher-Researcher Questions*

1. When we establish a community-of-learners atmosphere in the classroom, how can we define our instructional goals?
2. How can a lesson be redesigned to allow an investigative discovery approach?
3. What classroom communication behaviors might indicate that students have acquired a learned helplessness attitude toward their education?
4. When students are given the responsibility for questioning a text, what kinds of questions evolve?

## • *ACTIVITIES* •

### REFORMATTING QUESTIONS

OBJECTIVE: Students restructure textbook questions into an original format as a method of review and a means to generate new insights.

PROCESS: Ask students to reformat end-of-the-chapter-type questions into open-ended ones. For example, a textbook question after Chapter 7 of Book 2 of *A Tale of Two Cities*, by Charles Dickens, might read: "Who is the woman who stood knitting?" That question reformatted might look like: "How does the image of the woman knitting affect the meaning of this chapter?" Another example of a textbook-type question for Act 4 of *Romeo and Juliet* might be: "What is Juliet's reason for visiting the friar?" That question reformatted might be: "If Juliet were living today, to whom might she choose to go for help, and why?"

WHY THIS WORKS: As students reformat the questions, they review the material and the meanings. This activity can be done individually, with pairs, or in small groups. The reformatted questions can become a challenge for discussion and a prompt for writing.

## RECASTING QUESTIONS

OBJECTIVE: Students generate questions about a topic in order to foster investigative discourse.

PROCESS:

1. After completing a unit of work, such as a short story, novel, or drama, or before beginning a topic of discussion, students are asked to write "if" questions on the subject using the following forms:

   What if . . . ?

   How would you feel about _____ , if . . . ?

   How would you react to _____ , if . . . ?

   If you were _____ , what would you do, feel, think?

   If there were three times as many _____ , what would happen?

   *Samples:*

   a. If *Othello* were to be rewritten as a contemporary drama, what changes would you make in the characters and the situation?

   b. If you were to write the main character a letter, what would you advise him or her?

   c. If Ophelia did not commit suicide, how would the drama *Hamlet* be different?

   d. How would *Frankenstein* be different if it had been written by James Thurber?

2. Students form a circle and begin a discussion, preferably with a student leader. Three observers and the teacher listen and record the number of students' questions and comments. In turn, students ask one of their "if" questions. Other students respond to the questions with comments and ideas. These comments may also be spontaneous questions which arise from the discussion.

3. Criteria:

   a. Each student asks at least one question.

   b. Students maintain a questioning mode.

c. Students' questions are speculative rather than closed most of the time.

4. Evaluation Methods:

a. The teacher scores the number of oral questions and comments made by each person.

b. Students hand in written questions for credit.

c. Observers report their perceptions of the discussion.

WHY THIS WORKS: Students are encouraged to question in a risk-free atmosphere. Their "grade" depends only on the level of participation. As critical thinking, this method of projection means taking familiar material and recasting it in a new perspective.

*all good* IN-PROCESS QUESTIONING

OBJECTIVE: Students develop awareness of questions that surface as they process new material and they learn to value questioning while making meaning.

PROCESS:

1. After students have read silently for fifteen minutes, stop them. Say:

"Write down any questions that you have about the story (drama) right now. Can you visualize the setting? Do you know who all of the characters are? What questions might the author want you to think about?"

2. After the students have written their questions, direct them to read another fifteen minutes. Then tell students:

"Write projected answers to your first questions. Write three new questions based on where you have read thus far."

3. Divide the class into groups of four or five to discuss their questions and responses. After the small group sharing, a recorder reports back to the class their major questions and responses.

WHY THIS WORKS: This activity fosters metacognition. Students are made aware of the way their minds question as they read. They can set up their own hypotheses for the reasons behind certain actions. They can also make projections about the outcome of the plot without risk of "being wrong" as in a postreading assignment.

## CAPTURE THE PHRASE

OBJECTIVE: Students discover in the phrases of a literature selection the underlying meaning and significance of the words.

PROCESS:

1. Students read the first paragraph of a text. They select a phrase and think of all of the connections the words suggest.
2. They write a paragraph about the possible meanings and the ideas that are suggested.
3. Students pair with another classmate and discuss their individual ideas.
4. The whole class shares the ideas and predicts how these phrases and meanings will influence the story.
5. The class continues reading the story. Students note how many of their predictions come to pass.

WHY THIS WORKS: Students realize that vocabulary does more than tell a tale in literature. The introduction establishes the five *W*s of a story, but it also sets a mood. The activity allows students to discover the meanings and raises confidence and motivation for reading.

*Sample Selection*

Billy Weaver had traveled down from London on the slow afternoon train, with a change at Swindon on the way, and by the time he got to Bath it was about nine o'clock in the evening and the moon was coming up out of a clear starry sky over the houses opposite the station entrance. But the air was deadly cold and the wind was like a flat blade of ice on his cheeks. (From "The Landlady," by Roald Dahl 1985, p. 822)

# ● Three

· · · · · · · · · · · · · · · · ·

## The Questioning Class

> Questions themselves are not good or bad; patterns of questioning do, however, influence what will occur, with whom, in what ways, for what purposes, when, where, under what conditions, and with what short-term and long-term consequences.    —*Rogers, Green, and Nussbaum*

*E*stablishing a questioning class is challenging. Although most of us faced with a lost suitcase after a flight would not hesitate to ask the airline for help, we might not readily ask a question at a civic meeting or a public lecture. Each of us is affected by our feelings and the situation when we need to seek information. At risk is our self-concept. But other factors can impede our questioning. Faced with new situations, or lacking knowledge, we may not know *what* to ask, nor *when* we should ask. We cannot ask about the bus route, for instance, if we do not know that there is a bus.

Some people seem to naturally use questions in their interactions with others. Some do not. They prefer to find out information on their own. Nevertheless, since questioning builds meaning, makes connections between new knowledge and prior experience, and uncovers assumptions, we have a strong rationale to develop all students' abilities to question.

## Questioning Strategies

Some strategies can foster questioning: rearranging the physical environment, structuring more wait time, and forcing student-made questions are three beginning steps.

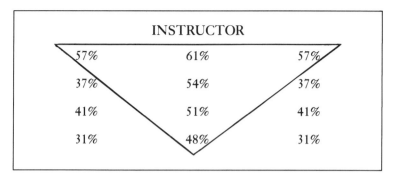

Figure 1: *Percentages of Participation  (Sommer 1969, 118)*

## Physical Environment

As feeling beings, we are influenced by physical factors in our surroundings. The classroom in which we teach has an impact on our communication behaviors. One study found a "soft" classroom with pastel colors, cushions, pictures on the wall, and carpets fostered more voluntary participation (79 percent) by students than the traditional classroom (51 percent) (Sommer and Olsen 1980).

### Furniture Arrangement

Arranging desks in rows affects participation. It has been found that students in the front and those in the center row participate to a greater degree than do those on the sides, with a pattern resembling a triangle (Figure 1). Simply rearranging the furniture, then, can produce better teacher-student dialogue. In addition, when students sit in rows they do not talk with each other, a strong rationale in the traditional structure. A teacher-centered communication system is not designed for student interaction. Students are discouraged from talk when they see only the backs of their classmates' heads. If we want to foster communication, they have to be able to see the other students' faces. A circle or a horseshoe encourages conversation. Even with the horseshoe, those students at the far end of the arrangement, opposite the teacher, have a tendency to participate more frequently than those on the sides. The teacher should make every effort to overcome those blind spots by deliberately including all students no matter where they sit.

## Wait Time

One of the simplest ways to encourage more reflection and questioning is to increase wait time. When teachers ask questions of students, they typically wait one second or less for students to reply. After a student responds the teacher begins the next question or her reaction in less than one second. Mary Budd Rowe (1986) has studied wait time for twenty years from elementary to college classes and from museum docent programs to special education classes. She has trained teachers to extend their wait time from less than one second to three or more seconds. Surprisingly, she has learned that teachers find this very difficult to do. Some are never able to wait longer than one second. Others can extend the wait time to as much as five seconds with positive results: self-initiated responses and questions increase, average length of responses increase, and failures to respond decrease. As speculative thinking increases, higher quality cognition is generated. Expanding wait time, in fact, decreases passivity. Instead of the estimated 30 percent "I don't know" or nonresponses in the usual teacher-student exchange, responses are raised to almost 100 percent.

David Perkins (1992) also suggests extending wait time. He recommends pausing until all the students have raised their hands and then calling on three people, discussing the differences in their answers. Wait time signals that the topic is worthy of thoughtful consideration. It also signals that the students' contributions are valued and important enough to be considered.

Changing the pace of classroom discourse appears simple, but it is not. Recitation is an entrenched habit for students and teachers. One of the strongest arguments for the quick dialogue is the need to "cover" the syllabus. The trap of coverage as a goal is that it denies both the teacher and the students the true adventure of learning. If we cover everything, most kids will not really understand, except in the most superficial way. Students need time to become deeply involved in a subject. They have to think about it in lots of ways and from lots of angles.

## Student-Made Questions

One method to increase participation is for the teacher to require student questions as part of the lesson. During a lecture, students can be asked to write down three questions every twenty minutes. The questions can be handled in different ways. They can be collected at the end of the class and answered within the next day's lecture. They can be responded to at the end of class on the same day, or they can form the basis of an informal discussion.

Students can be asked to write questions about a text before they come to class. As an example, students in a twelfth grade class studying "The Witness" by Doris Lessing were asked to devise three questions about the text. Their questions could be factual if they needed specific information, but since these questions were to be used for a class discussion, speculative questions were more desirable. Sample student questions were:

Why does Mr. Brooke have his dog? His canary?
How do you feel Marnie felt doing odd jobs? Why was she
   doing odd jobs?
Why do you think Mr. Brooke was so attached to Marnie?

Each of these questions may signal comprehension problems, but they also contain potential for exploration into deeper meanings. Student-made questions, beginning as they do nearer to students' level of understanding, permit better access into meaning than do teacher-made questions. The following transcript of a class discussion reveals how an apparently simple question triggers a metaphoric comparison:

STUDENT 1: Why does Mr. Brooke have his dog and canary?
STUDENT 2: Mainly for company. Let me think—no other people
would talk to him, so—

STUDENT 3: But did his dog and his canary really talk to him?

STUDENT 4: Didn't he say how like—

STUDENT 5: Not stupid, but how dumb they were—or something—it was to have them—

STUDENT 1: Do you think that he just had them to get attention from other people?

STUDENT 5: He had them because there was nobody else. I mean he had them to talk to.

STUDENT 3: But didn't he say that—he also said that—it was kind of like a night light for a little kid that he had them so like a little kid likes to have a night light on because they're afraid of the dark, and I guess he was kind of afraid of being alone, so he had his dog and his canary.

The complexity of comprehension becomes readily apparent through this discussion. What begins as a simple question evolves into a symbolic discussion of human motivations. The example of a night light for a child reveals the aching loneliness of a neglected man. Identifying a character's behaviors with one's own experience creates a meaning beyond the words of a text. Questioning and probing helps students to construct connections to their own lives.

## Reducing Nonresponses

Student questions are an effective way to reduce nonresponses. Because the discussion begins with the students' level of knowledge, they have something to contribute. A helpful strategy to increase participation is to credit in some fashion all student contributions, whether written or oral. One ninth grade teacher uses a point system during class discussions. She scores the number of times students speak. Those with nothing new to offer receive a point if they say, "I agree with [another student's] answer because [reason for agreement]." This reinforces the pattern of giving a response and not passing. Often, their reasons turn out to be original, or provide a new slant on the topic. These tactics, and others listed later in this chapter, are intended to increase participation. The theory is that the more students question, the more active their participation, the better the learning that they will experience.

# *Quality of Questions*

One pedagogical issue remains, however. So what if students are questioning more—what about the quality of the questions? To a certain degree, there is validity in the belief that the level of questioning affects the level of resultant thinking. Observe your own thinking as you read the following questions about the nursery tale "The Three Little Pigs."

1. Who was threatening the three little pigs?
2. What material did the first little pig use in building his house?
3. How are the three little pigs like you?
4. How might the story have been different if the wolf had been a rat?
5. How can you turn the story into a poem?
6. If you change the ending of the story, how will it affect the meaning?

Each question calls into play certain cognitive functions, some more complex than others. Recalling information may have less status than analysis in the hierarchy of cognition, but nevertheless it is an essential element in the thinking process. We need facts. Recall questions are not wrong or bad. They just should not be the only kind of question asked.

Some scholars advocate structuring questions in such a way as to promote higher-order thinking. Particularly favored are those derived from logic or argumentation.

1. What claims are being made?
2. Are the claims valid?
3. What evidence is presented to support the claim?
4. How credible is the source of information?

Questioning in this manner creates interesting perspectives on character analysis. For instance, how credible is Macbeth as a source when he says to Duncan:

The service and the loyalty I owe,
In doing pays itself. Your Highness' part
Is to receive our duties.

*45*

And one could debate the validity of the claim made by the apparitions in the play, as reported by Macbeth:

> The spirits that know
> All mortal consequences have pronounced me thus:
> "Fear not Macbeth. No man that's born of woman
> Shall e'er have power upon thee."

However, once we realize that learning is cyclical and not linear, we can be more assured that questioning procedures do not have to follow a prescriptive order of difficulty.

## Interactive Thinking

Probably the most important kind of intervention that the teacher can use is to model an investigative approach to knowledge. Smagorinsky and Fly (1993) report the desirability of this form of discourse in their study. We can audiotape our own classroom discussions as a monitor of the kinds of questions and interventions that work for us. The following transcript of a discussion about "The Rain Horse" by Ted Hughes illustrates a teacher's attempt to help students probe more deeply:

TEACHER: So who is he angry with?

LORA: Himself.

TEACHER: He is angry with himself?

ANNA: Yeah.

TEACHER: Why is he angry with himself?

ANNA: For not coming back for twelve years.

TEACHER: For not coming back for twelve years?

KATHY: Maybe he thought coming back after twelve years, he stayed away that long maybe something was there, and he was going back. And then he stayed away for twelve years, cause he was ashamed, and he did something really bad when he was there—something like that—

ANNA: Then he sees the horse and started thinking he should leave—get away. Then he started seeing the horse—first paragraph and in the second paragraph.

TEACHER: Where is the first time he sees the horse?

TRACI: Right after he—

ANNA: "Over to his right a thin, black horse was running"—The first paragraph on page 57.

TEACHER: So, the horse appears when his emotion is high, like the anger has come up in him?

ANNA: He feels that he should leave quickly.

TEACHER: Have you ever felt not welcome in any situation and an outcast? Or have you ever had a memory from your childhood that would make you feel this way?

KATHY: Yeah, but what I was going to say is that, like talking about he felt unwelcome in the land that maybe he had done something wrong and maybe that's why he was seeing the horse— like mentally torturing himself because he knew he had done wrong and he shouldn't be there so maybe that's why he imagined the horse to be behaving that way and so like it's "Oh no! A warning!" or something to get out of the land—to don't come back.

The teacher's questions prompt more speculation and a movement from concrete descriptions to more abstract interpretations. The questions were not constructed from a hierarchal model of difficulty. The interaction of the participants became a catalyst for more complex thought.

## Taxonomy

Levels of abstractions are often defined categorically by different authors. Theoretically, students who mindfully learn methods of analysis, synthesis, and evaluation, among other skills, will become more effective thinkers.

The drawbacks from conceptualizing thought in this way are:

1. An assumption is made that one method is superior to another.
2. Only one method at a time is, or should be, employed.
3. The thought process has linearity.

The truth is that we use all functions concurrently—one is not superior to another—nor do we necessarily process information in identical patterns regardless of the situation. The danger of trying to force questions into a hierarchal mode, whether teacher-made or student-made, is that no evidence indicates that better critical thinking is elicited specifically from one category over another. Hierarchies should be viewed as descriptive of cognitive processes rather than as prescriptive. In fact, despite claims otherwise, numerous studies have been unable to definitively classify the hierarchal level of questions in actual classroom discussions (Christenbury and Kelly 1983).

Too often, proponents of critical thinking "sell" the idea by promoting a hierarchy of skills that must be taught in a precise manner. Following rigid guidelines and doing particular exercises to develop a skill is the complete opposite of critical thinking—where one is able to view many alternate possibilities.

Nevertheless, teachers are often exhorted to include questions that call on higher order thinking skills by designing them to fit a taxonomy such as Bloom's (1979). Crafting questions to fit such a format are instructive and fun. For a lesson in literature, the questions might look like these for a lesson on *Romeo and Juliet*.

*Knowledge:* What threat does Prince Escalus make to the Capulets and the Montagues in Act I of *Romeo and Juliet?*

*Comprehension:* How does Mercutio's Queen Mab speech contribute to understanding the situation or the characters?

*Application:* How does the feud between the Capulets and the Montagues compare to current situations in the world?

*Analysis:* In your opinion is Romeo justified in avenging Mercutio's death or should he have allowed Prince Escalus to have dealt with it?

*Synthesis:* What aspects of Juliet and Romeo's lives contribute most to their tragedy: their youth, their passion, the family feud, their social status, their friends or relations, or chance?

*Evaluation:* Has *Romeo and Juliet* been popular through the centuries merely because it is a love story, or has its social message contributed to its appeal as well?

Now look back at the transcript of the discussion of "The Rain Horse." Although, by construction, the questions were deceptively simple, the kinds of thought processes could be compared to the taxonomy above. For instance, the teacher's question, "So, who is he angry with?" can be ranked on the factual or literal level, or it can be ranked on the interpretive or comprehension level. "Why is he angry with himself?" can be inferential, the analytical level, or it can also be hypothetical, categorized as the synthesis level. "For not coming back for twelve years?" can similarly be categorized as comprehension, analysis, or even, perhaps, knowledge. Each of these nondirective questions, by themselves, are not structures of complexity. It is the stimulation of the discussion that draws upon certain cognitive elements. The context of the discourse, or environmental domain, shapes thinking more than the semantic structure of the questions themselves.

## Dynamics of Questioning

When we look at the answers students gave, we find they make speculations about possible interpretations. Although Anna returns to the text for "knowledge," rereading a paragraph from page 57, no definitive answer is achieved. In "The Rain Horse," as in most texts, multiple interpretations are possible because of the space the author gives the reader. The questions, and the mode of discussion, allow a picture to grow of a man and a situation. There is a filling out of a scene only vaguely described by the author.

Another interesting fact that I discovered about this kind of discussion is that when no closure is reached, unanswered questions surface days later. The mind keeps working on puzzles. A postwriting by Veeta reveals her ongoing processing of this story's meaning. It also reveals how the external questioning of the discussion becomes one of her internal methods of discovery.

> "The Rain Horse" was what a lot of people would say or call an unsolved mystery. The story is telling you in full detail how a man is reacting to a horse he says is following him, also how hard it is raining. The story never did come out and say whether or not the horse was real or imaginary for that matter. It also refuses to tell us about whether or not the man was just walking down the street to get a few things off his mind, or whether he was looking for something specific.
>
> But I guess that is what makes it interesting when you have to look, think, question, discuss, and read. It all seems it would be a dream, but if you think about it, it just might be real. I mean, let's think of the situations and the problems it has in it. First, why would he be walking in the rain in a two-piece outfit? Secondly, why would he walk so far from home? And, thirdly, why would the horse chase him like a mad horse if he hadn't done anything to harm him?

Another student, Kathy, who has more language facility, conceptualizes the horse in a more symbolic manner.

> The man is feeling confused and frustrated in the last paragraph of the story. He is wondering if, in fact, the incident with the horse was real. For the first time he is skeptical of the situation that occurred. . . . In the paragraph it says "as if some important part had been cut out of his brain," shows that even he had doubts as to the state of his sanity or his mental capacity. . . . This one phrase helps to support our discussion of the story and our beliefs of the man's abnormalities. . . . The horse was a sign or an omen of some sort because of the situation that had occurred twelve years before. The horse was meant to show that he wasn't welcome there now and, perhaps, never would be. This is the root of the anxiety and utter disbelief he is feeling, the part of his brain that is missing is quite possibly the part that holds his memories of the past.

In Kathy's writing the questions are not directly stated. Nevertheless, their presence is implicit in her explication. Questions, when they are student-made, have a prolonged life because they arise from the core of their construct systems rather than being superimposed.

In addition, the whole notion of teacher questioning as providing superior thinking is challenged by the results of research undertaken by Jerry Feezel (1989). Feezel found that high school students saw teacher questions in actual classroom transcripts as demanding lower levels of thinking than did either the author of the questions or teacher raters. Thus, Feezel says, "It is possible we are overrating the thinking demands of our questions or underrating the abilities of our students to think" (p. 3).

## *Scaffolding*

Teachers, consciously or unconsciously, model a form of questioning by their attitudes toward inquiry. Students have also absorbed a repertoire of classroom-type questions in their memory banks. However, relying on habitual methods may not meet the challenge of developing questions to deepen thinking abilities. Scaffolds, or forms of support, assist learners when they have to make a bridge between the unknown and the known. Scaffolds, as the name suggests, are temporary structures that can be abandoned or dismantled as learner proficiency increases (Applebee and Langer 1984).

We can think of scaffolds as generative, procedural, or evaluative. Generative strategies are prompts to assist writing, thinking, and questioning. Specific words and phrases can help formulate questions: who, what, where, when, why, how, what if, to what extent, how often, what are the alternatives, and what else do I need to know? Activities at the end of this chapter, as well as those at the end of other chapters, offer examples of scaffolding prompts.

Procedural scaffolding is the way we go about setting up the classroom, from the arrangement of furniture to the grouping of students. Learning task and maintenance responsibilities is a form of scaffolding. As students become proficient in their use, rules can be relaxed or modified depending on the need or task. The whole process of discussion, sharing ideas, listening, and withholding critical judgments, are also kinds of scaffolding.

Evaluative scaffolding involves checking the ongoing process of questioning. Students can self-monitor their progress through journals, checklists, talking with peers, observations, and debriefing discussions in small groups or the whole class. The overall goal of scaffolding is that these external methods will become internalized as useful behaviors for the individual. We should not think of scaffolding as appropriate for only underachieving students. All of us have a need for scaffolding when we embark on difficult or unfamiliar tasks. It resembles the novice learning to use pitons and crampons under the guidance of a more experienced rock climber.

As students become more proficient with questioning, they develop a scaffolding of their own. From my observation of classroom discourse, when students are given investigative tasks, they can form structures to support these tasks, provided they have had ample practice in discussion techniques and responsibilities.

## Investigative Discourse

We should not think of classroom questioning in terms of the courtroom or argumentation. It is more productive if we view it as investigative rather than adversarial inquiry. Questioning if it is shaped as argument often engenders anger. Open-ended question-making, on the other hand, leads to higher-level abstract thinking, without presuming an adversary. Scaffolding for question-generation and investigative responses promotes free discussion. It draws on students' previous knowledge as they originate questions. Reviewing information, applying it to new situations, and testing perceptions against classmates' answers advances communication skills and improves cognitive complexity in ways that do not have to be confrontational. Questioning in an investigative climate is marked by a supportive stance. Students question each other for mutual gain, not to win. The structure permits the lower achiever equal access to the discussion, since all questions and answers are potentially important for understanding. Generative thinking thrives in an open forum where we value the worth of everyone's ideas.

*Teacher-Researcher Questions*

1. How might restructuring the physical environment influence teacher-student and student-student interaction?
2. What effect does altering wait time have on student response?
3. If students generate questions while they are reading a text, how will their learning be affected?
4. What procedural scaffolding would assist in reducing students' nonresponsive behavior?

## • *ACTIVITIES* •

### CHARACTER QUESTIONS

OBJECTIVE: Students are allowed the opportunity to develop their cognitive complexity and the ability to decenter, or to move away from an egocentric view, through thinking in the role of a character.

PROCESS:

1. After reading a text, ask students to imagine they are one of the characters and to write three questions as that character. The first question is to the author about the way their character behaves or is treated. The second is to another character about his/her behavior or attitude. And the third is to the reader about his or her reactions to the character. All questions should be written in the language and tone of the chosen character.
2. Students pass the questions to the person on their left. Each person answers the first question in the role of the author.

3. They pass the questions again to the left. This time each person assumes the persona of the character addressed to write a response.
4. Now, they pass the question for a third time, answering the new question as a reader of the story or drama.
5. The questions are returned to the original writers. The class divides into groups to discuss the questions and the responses. Now students assume their original roles, as they read their questions and the responses that they received.
6. When they all have shared their answers, the groups report to the whole class what they observed about the kinds of responses and what increased understandings they have gained.

WHY THIS WORKS: Students experiment with thoughts and language from a variety of perspectives. They are freed from the usual character, plot, and setting analysis questions and can find multiple avenues for making meaning.

## QUESTIONING MEANING

OBJECTIVES: Students explore the meaning of literary texts by questioning motives, actions, and intent of characters. They can also explore their impressions of situations and the seeming perplexity of interrelated events.

PROCESS:

1. Students are directed to write three questions about a literary work that they are studying. They do not have to know the answers to these questions. The questions may be open-ended or factual. For Conrad's *Heart of Darkness*, for instance, questions might be:

   Why is Marlow unable to repair his steamboat?
   Why does Marlow say that he sees "truth" when he looks at the African natives?

2. Next students select one of their questions and write a one-page response. They can begin by saying, "I don't really

understand this . . . ," but then they can develop a speculative answer. These questions, then, become the basis of a small group discussion, a personal reading journal, a panel discussion, or a group presentation for the class.

WHY THIS WORKS: Constructing questions encourages students to move beyond passivity into reflection. Sometimes their speculative questions provide a hypothesis from which they can test a number of assumptions; e.g., "Is Scobie really evil or corrupt in the novel *The Heart of the Matter?*" But questions can relate to literal problems, too. For instance, they might learn that Frances dies of tuberculosis in *Wuthering Heights* when they ask: "What is consumption?"

## QUESTIONS! QUESTIONS! QUESTIONS!

OBJECTIVE: Students develop their ability to generate questions concerning relationships, reordering of information, and inferring meanings of words and relationships.

PROCESS:

1. Students are given a poem such as Sonnet 141 by Shakespeare.

> In faith, I do not love thee with mine eyes,
> For they in thee a thousand errors note;
> But 'tis my heart that loves what they despise,
> Who in despite of view is pleased to dote;
> Nor are mine ears with thy tongue's tune delighted,
> Nor tender feeling, to base touches prone,
> Nor taste, nor smell, desire to be invited
> To any sensual feast with thee alone:
> But my five wits nor my five senses can
> Dissuade one foolish heart from serving thee,
> Who leaves unsway'd the likeness of a man,
> The proud hearts slave and vassal wretch to be:
> Only my plague thus far I count my gain,
> That she that makes me sin awards me pain.

2. Students first read the poem silently. Then either volunteers can read the poem aloud, or, with the teacher modeling the reading of the first line, students can read it aloud a line at a time.

3. Students are then asked to look the poem over and write three questions. They may be "if" questions, "how would" questions, "why" questions, or questions based on images or words.

4. Next, students select one of their questions and write a response to it.

5. The class divides into small groups. One person in the group reads the poem aloud again. Then each person in the group asks one of his or her questions of the group.

6. After everyone in the group responds, the questioner gives his or her own answer. They continue in this manner until all of the questions have been asked, or until the allotted time has ended. The group selects their best question to bring back to the whole class, but they list the rest of their questions.

7. Students return to a large class circle, with each small group sitting together. One person from each group asks the class their best question. And that group, in turn, leads the discussion. If another group has thought of the same question as their first choice, other options remain since each group has a number of questions. Oftentimes, although the questions are similar, the responses are quite different, and thus worthy of repetition.

WHY THIS WORKS: The variety of ideas this kind of discussion provokes helps students to learn to approach poetry from a variety of angles. The different interpretation of words or images fills out the meaning and prevents the understanding from being a textbook exercise.

## READING CHECK QUESTIONS

OBJECTIVE: Students determine understanding of reading assignments through student-made questions.

PROCESS:

1. This idea is an adaptation of Frye's (1992) "Quiz Bowl." Teams of students concoct questions based on daily reading assignments.
2. They turn in their written questions and answers and conduct the questioning as leaders of the discussion. This format allows them to practice leadership skills in discussion and to review major concepts.

WHY THIS WORKS: Students have an opportunity to ask questions on their own level and to explore meanings. Again the atmosphere is nonthreatening because the value is placed on the development of questions and the responses to them, not on the recall of factual information.

## MEDIA QUESTIONS

OBJECTIVE: Students learn to evaluate television news and formulate questions regarding the media's coverage of news events.

PROCESS:

1. This idea is an adaptation of Tolar's (1992) "My Favorite Newsteam: Comparative Analysis of the Nightly News." Students are divided into groups to watch network news. They are instructed to note the topics, coverage, and depth of analysis. They are also asked to devise questions that one should ask about the news coverage to determine its adequacy of topic coverage, fairness in choice of evidence, and sufficiency in quality and quantity of sources.
2. Students present their observation of the news programs as groups. The groups assigned to other networks ask questions about the completeness, bias, and depth of the information covered.
3. A useful follow-up is to show a C-SPAN clip of the same topic as was reported on the nightly news. Students can question any contrasts between their newsteam's coverage and information from primary sources.

<u>WHY THIS WORKS</u>: Students are encouraged not only to watch but also to evaluate the quality of the news coverage by a particular network. They can develop a sense of the editorial strengths and weaknesses demonstrated by the station they watched, and they can begin to evaluate video news in general. This activity draws on the familiar medium of television that students generally favor over the print media. Thus this activity provides a contrast to the usual classroom emphasis on print media.

# ● *Four*

· · · · · · · · · · · · · · · · ·

## *Whole Class Discussion*

True group discussion is rare. . . . Even activities that
teachers call "discussion" tend to be recitations in which
teachers ask questions and students respond by reciting
what they already know or are presently learning.
                                              —*Good and Brophy*

*I* ronically, although most teachers would claim that
they have whole class discussions, or even Socratic dialogues,
the truth is that both are rare. Study after study indicates that
teachers dominate discussion and are largely unaware of their
communication behavior.

When we listen to this twelfth grade class discuss
"Peaches," by Dylan Thomas, we can observe the teacher's
role in the discussion. Instead of telling the students what they
should notice about the characters, she chooses to use questions.

STUDENT 1: Alcoholism is a problem.

STUDENT 2: Right. If he wanted a better life, he wouldn't be
drinking all the time—he would try and stop.

STUDENT 3: Maybe he drinks because there is something in his
life that he doesn't want to face.

TEACHER: What is that?

STUDENT 4: Reality.

TEACHER: When you say reality, that is general. I want to know
what specifics could lead to this.

STUDENT 5: They're poor and it messes up the family.

STUDENT 2: I think it's poverty.

STUDENT 6: I think he wants more for his family, but he can't get it and I think he just wants to hide it. You know by the way he is going.

TEACHER: What does he want besides the poverty? What else? Is that the major thing? Money?

STUDENT 7: He wants to be happy.

The teacher doesn't dictate an answer or an approach. She raises nonjudgmental questions as an aid for them to probe more deeply for meanings. They are asked to look at the reasons for their responses. It appears that the students and the teacher are working together as a group in order to share opinions and to arrive at an understanding.

## *Whole Class Seminar Discussion*

Researchers document that in 84 percent of classroom communication events teachers are the principal actors. That teachers are so dominant may not be too disturbing until we discover that the way information is being processed is primarily through recall. One study, involving 300 hours of observation in reading and social studies classrooms, found that only 3 hours, or 1 percent of the time, was related to comprehension instruction (Good and Brophy 1991). And, although teachers believe they employ Socratic questioning, observers report its use only a fraction of the time.

In order to conduct discussions that will build understanding and evoke higher-order thinking, teachers must radically alter their traditional methods. They must learn to structure discussions where they can play a less dominant role. As facilitators, they can establish a focus, set boundaries, and design a workable environment.

Teachers must also learn to tolerate the slower pace of real discussion as opposed to the speed of recitations. Expressive speech, with its tentativeness, spontaneity, and loose structure, is not as linear as teacher-directed discourse. Participants pause longer, reflect on meanings, and consider possible responses.

These behaviors allow a more thought-filled exchange, but those silences make both teachers and students nervous.

Attempting to lead whole class discussions can be discouraging. Large classes thwart real dialogue between the teacher and the pupils under the best of circumstances. "Discussions" can become monologues or conversations with only one or two vocal students. False discussions are doubly dangerous. First, they give the impression that discussion, even Socratic discussion, is taking place. Second, students are cheated out of the opportunity for higher cognitive thought. Therefore it is imperative to give up the idea that teacher dominance is the only way to direct discussion.

## Seminars

Lectures are a form of teaching by telling, or didactic teaching. Seminars are different. "It is teaching by asking and by a discussion conducted through questions asked and answered and with answers often disputed" (Adler 1983, 167). Seminars conducted in this manner are rare occurrences in schools, even through college.

Seminars, or true discussions, can be considered almost a revolutionary way to teach. Teachers, for the most part, have not been trained in communication nor have they participated in seminars until graduate classes. Neither have their students experienced true discussion with its attendant responsibilities in other classes. And that goes to the heart of the problem. Responsibility for discussion rests on *all* of the participants, not just the teacher. Everyone comes prepared for a seminar. Television panelists illustrate the expected interaction. All of the guests contribute information or insights. No one is there to just fill a seat and smile for the camera. That same level of preparation produces lively seminars in the classroom.

## Moderator Qualities

The success of a seminar begins with the leader. If the teacher is not going to dominate the discussion, what should her role be? It helps to envision the task as a moderator: that most interesting, and sometimes frustrating, role. Teachers complain, "How can my students discuss the literature if they haven't read the assignment!" They report, "Half of the students won't talk, or speak so softly they can't be heard." Or, "They know so little about the topic, it's the blind leading the blind." The moderator's task is to draw out information and to guide interpretations of material without predetermined answers in mind. The first qualification, then, for a successful moderator is to have trust in the participants and in the process. The moderator must be comfortable with ambiguities and the possibility of more than one answer, since a seminar is not a place where one "discusses" the correctness of the equation $2 + 3 = 5$. Seminar topics are about issues, ideas, values, and shades of meaning. The topics are most exciting if they are somewhat controversial, if differing viewpoints are offered, and if they lend themselves to multiple interpretations.

The moderator must be a careful listener, "reading" the intent as well as the message. As a critical listener, the moderator must notice and remember contradictions or discrepancies in information and use those to further explorations, not through direct challenges, but through guided questioning. The teacher in this segment of a transcript of a class discussion of "The Rain Horse" by Ted Hughes attempts to guide student thinking:

TEACHER: Why do you think [the protagonist] is thirty?

STUDENT 1: Because if he was older, he wouldn't be that energetic to run that thing.

STUDENT 2: The way he talked and the way he dresses, kinda like a yuppie, you know.

STUDENT 3: I thought maybe he was old and senile.

TEACHER: It says that he has his anxiety about shoes and his new suit and so forth. Does this sort of suggest somebody who hasn't had that many suits or that many shoes?

STUDENT 1: Well, maybe he has just been out of style.

TEACHER: And just now has the money to buy the new shoes and suit?

The questions keep options open and allow for reversals and reevaluation of information.

The moderator's role as a questioner is probably the most difficult, although the type of question is not as important as an open climate. Astute insights are born from seemingly mundane questions, or even in response to statements. The full responsibility for ideas does not depend on the moderator, as this exchange illustrates:

> STUDENT MODERATOR: What kind of person do you think Marnie was [in "The Witness," by Doris Lessing]?
>
> STUDENT 1: Well, I think she wasn't very sure. She didn't belong in the world of business. She didn't want to leave home, and she was very lonely.
>
> STUDENT 2: It seems like it was okay for her to make a mistake— like to mess up a file and that infuriated the other ladies. They felt she could get away with a lot more than anybody else and she knew it.

## Moderator Tasks

The role of moderator does not have to be performed only by the teacher. Leadership is not an attribute of age, status, or natural talent. It is part of the skill of communication that we should teach. We can view the tasks of the moderator as threefold:

1. To direct the flow of questions and answers in a productive manner.
2. To examine the responses by trying to probe for their reasons or their implications.
3. To encourage the participants to respond to each other when the views they present appear to be in conflict.

The third task, encouraging participants to talk to one another, is especially challenging. Generally, the moderator's immediate reaction is to respond directly to a speaker, rather than to channel the comment to another participant. If the moderator does bounce a speaker's idea to another group member, there are some pitfalls. Calling on someone by name requires, at least in our culture, an automatic answer. We feel an obligation to speak when we are addressed specifically. Creating that obligation, thus, ensures a reaction. Unfortunately, the reaction can be negative. Students can feel put on the spot or threatened, diminishing the climate of trust.

On the other hand, the moderator should carefully read nonverbal signals from participants, noting signs that students want to speak. Acknowledging these individuals by name allows them entry into the discussion. Another factor that helps foster interaction is to pause after questions or responses. In other words, the moderator works to increase a tolerance for *productive silence*. The best ideas need gestation time. Rushing headlong from one thought to another prevents the kind of reflection that advances knowledge.

Because leadership should be shared with students, they need to learn to practice it responsibly. They should be informed of leadership tasks and practice those behaviors as members of a discussion. The following guidelines will help in understanding the leader's role.

### Leadership Task Guidelines

These tasks are the special jobs of discussion leaders, but all members should assume responsibility if the group is to function well. The leader:

1. Initiates discussion.
2. Allows members the equal right to speak.
3. Keeps the group on topic.
4. Focuses on issues.
5. Probes for answers.
6. Summarizes the conclusions of the group.
7. Maintains control.
   (Adapted from O'Keefe 1988a, 15)

## Student Responsibility

While the leader must fulfill certain tasks for a successful discussion, he or she can go only as far as the capabilities of the participants. While it is one thing to say that students should be prepared for a seminar, it is quite another to ensure that it happens. For collaborative learning to take place, it is necessary for students to accept their share of "speaker decisions." For this level of interaction to occur it is important to develop students' skills, confidence, and communication ability. The first steps are to help students learn the various strategies for effective communication and the functions of discussion, including the role of moderator. They need to learn to create and ask nonjudgmental questions such as:

What does this suggest?
If the sequence of events were changed, how would that affect the story?
What parts could you combine?
How does X relate to Y?
Where are the contradictions?
How does the context change the meaning?

They need a chance to "practice" seminar discussion in small groups. Verbalizing their ideas first in a less threatening environment helps students overcome their reluctance to speak and helps them refine their ideas. It's less of a risk to express a thought before a whole class if they have had a chance to experiment first with a few friends.

Students need to feel comfortable in an atmosphere of inquiry. They need to learn to take responsibility not only for preparing work in advance but also for speaking during the discussion. They must ask questions, make hypotheses, check information, and summarize major findings. The teacher may shift from moderator to participant or observer. Still her role is a vital one. Her responsibility is to structure the communication process and to design assignments that foster constructive dialogue.

## *Preparing for Discussion*

As language arts teachers, we often use talk as preparation for the product of writing: brain storming sessions, buzz groups, writer-reader responses. What I suggest is to use writing to improve talk. When students write ideas, questions, or informal journals prior to discussion, each person has something to say. Having something in hand increases confidence and contributions. The three *P*s can be guidelines: Preparation, Practice, and Playback.

### Preparation

1. Each individual has some type of prediscussion responsibility. He or she may be assigned to make notes in a journal, do free writing, produce written responses to readings, or research background information for the group discussion.
2. Students discuss aloud the demands of the task.

### Practice

1. Each individual presents his or her ideas in an equitable manner within a small group.
2. Group members respond in turn with constructive comments, questions, or requests for more information. In this way, students practice the skills of listening, sharing, and valuing others' comments.

### Playback

1. Students report to the class as a whole through informal or formal presentations.
2. Students write in journals or produce free responses.
3. Class members ask questions or expand on the ideas.
   (Adapted from O'Keefe 1988a, 13–14)

Discussions do not occur in an empty space. We talk about something. The most valuable discussions take place about important subjects. One way to generate dialogue is to show a controversial short film or a C-SPAN video of congressional debate. Using the three *P*s as a guideline, have students begin by writing a ten-minute free response about the issue. Before beginning discussion, hand out the Leadership Task Guidelines list (mentioned earlier).

## Preparation and Practice

Divide the class into small groups to "practice" discussion. Each group selects a recorder to write down interesting ideas. Everyone should speak as the group prepares a list of their combined ideas. Students practice leadership by asking others for feedback and initiating discussion as they share their writings. This balanced sharing is extremely important.

One way to achieve equality is to ask students to label themselves by the letters A, B, C, D, and E in the small groups. First A speaks and the others respond, then B speaks and so forth. This method forestalls one person dominating the group. And since every member of the group has a "product" to share, everyone is likely to contribute.

After fifteen minutes or so, it is time to pause and evaluate the process. The groups should study the leadership tasks and discuss how well their group fulfilled those duties. This process may take about five minutes. As a follow-up, students write journals assessing the experience, focusing particularly on their own behavior.

## Playback

Now it is time for Playback. In a traditional fifty-minute class, the preceding activity has probably occupied most of the time. Therefore, Playback takes place the next day. Collect the recorders' lists from each group. Appoint moderators for the seminar discussion, one from each group. Dividing leadership diminishes fear and the responsibility of individuals. Groups generate questions on the topic to ask the other groups.

The next day when the class assembles, arrange the seats in a circle or a square so that everyone can have eye contact with everyone else. The appointed moderators sit in the front of the room, while the groups sit together around the circle or square. The moderators lead the discussion when their group is reporting; however, that rule does not have to be followed strictly. Each leader has a copy of the list of ideas and questions that his or her group generated, which assists in the monitoring of the discussion.

This leadership experience and training cannot be overemphasized. Girls and minorities may not have had much opportunity to lead. The Sadkers (1993) report that the reticence of girls to initiate comments or to assume leadership roles may have been learned early in school. We need to put aside assumptions about who is capable of leading. There is an added benefit in "practicing" leadership. Sitting in front of the room trying to get classmates to participate makes the problem of stimulating good discussion abundantly clear. Walking in the teacher's shoes helps students to appreciate both the value of discussion and the need for everyone to contribute. Leadership should be rotated frequently in discussion sessions.

Kathy, a senior, talks about what occurs when these roles are not taught.

> I think they should start [group discussion training] as early as elementary school. . . . Let them be a leader of a discussion group—something like that because generally when teachers put you in a discussion group, they will pick on someone who they know is already a leader, so they are going to pick them just because they have leadership qualities, but how do they get leadership qualities? Teachers have designated certain people since kindergarten and that is not fair to other people. Just like they have stuff here with leadership conferences, and they always pick the same people for them. I mean, how do they know that there aren't other people out there who can be leaders?

In answer to Kathy's question, *they* don't know who can be leaders because leadership is not taught. Whose responsibility is it to teach leadership? I believe it is the responsibility of language arts teachers, because we are a verbal culture and we perceive leaders as having verbal qualities. Practicing communication as leaders in a seminar discussion develops the mind and the capabilities of all students.

Individual students should be appointed as summarizers. They listen to the discussion and periodically recapitulate major ideas for the class. They also provide closure at the end of the discussion. Their observations help to focus on the major points as an aid to all of the students when they reflect on the meanings.

Following the discussion, students write informally about their reactions to the controversial issue that served as the prompt to the lesson.

In order for discussion to have a strong purpose, even during the training stage, it helps to relate the subject to the literature or composition topics under consideration. When studying *Of Mice and Men*, for example, issues could be the Great Depression, mental retardation, or labor problems. Tying process and product together creates a momentum for learning.

## More Practice

Discussions such as these need to be repeated often, giving students numerous chances to participate actively and learn the various roles. We do not become expert ice skaters after one turn on the ice. Many opportunities for discussion surface during the school year. School elections, graduation requirements, career choices, student parking regulations, athletic eligibility, social concerns, current events, as well as literature are all fruitful subjects. We send the message with open forums that our classrooms are part of the students' society. Literature grapples with reality. It is not "out there." The reason the literary canon survives is that it speaks to us generation after generation, not because of English teachers and their dedication to the archaic. To avoid repetitiveness, the structure can be altered and writing prompts varied.

From the description of a seminar discussion it becomes readily apparent that the process is more time consuming than traditional methods. Time is a precious commodity in the classroom. How then can seminar discussion be justified? Concept building is not a speedy task. Speaking-to-learn and writing-to-learn activities deservedly should occupy a significant amount of time. If we omit them, we may cover more facts, but gain mere superficial understanding. Valuing the learning process and granting time for students' ideas to evolve require the teacher's patience. But the process of learning must also be continually reevaluated. We have to ask ourselves questions. Is this writing generating substance? Are students gaining new insights?

Teaching students the functions of a leader, as well as those of a member, does not imply that the teacher should never take on the role of moderator. Modeling leadership extends horizons of learning as the participants become more active and experience successful group action. Nevertheless, this role differs from the one that the teacher traditionally plays in the classroom in one important way. The moderator does not take the position of knowing more than the students. Teachers as moderators are simply more competent learners than the students.

## Socratic Questioning

Discussion as a way to enlarge ideas is not a substitute for the acquisition of information from direct instruction, however. The teacher must combine the roles of lecturer, guide, and expert interpreter. These functions, along with textbooks and related materials, are the means by which students acquire information. Seminar discussion is the application and development of that information into a more meaningful, and thus more permanent, context.

If the teacher-moderator chooses Socratic questioning, then it helps to examine both what it is and what it is not. Mortimer Adler (1983, 172) explains what it is not.

> It is not a quiz session in which a teacher asks Yes or No questions and says Right or Wrong to the answers. . . .
>
> It is not a lecture in disguise in which the teacher asks questions and, after a brief pause or after listening to one or two unsatisfactory responses, then proceeds to answer his own questions at

length, thus in effect giving a lecture that is punctuated by the questions asked. . . .

It is not a glorified "bull session" in which everyone feels equally free to express opinions on the level of personal prejudices or to recount experiences that the narrator of them regards as highly significant of something or other.

One warning should be observed regarding Adler's admonition that personal experiences are irrelevant. Eliminating that kind of response denies us one of the important ways to make sense of the world. While it is true that taking a rambling trip through someone's memories may be counterproductive to critical thinking, examples of personal experience illuminate and exemplify information for the speaker and the listener. The moderator needs to control but not squelch that kind of response.

A more inclusive idea of Socratic questioning fits the purpose of this book. Questioning can originate from the teacher, student, or self. The only requirement is that the thoughts developed are a result of stimulating questions.

If a student says that people are selfish, the teacher may wonder aloud as to what it means to say that, how the student explains acts others call altruistic, what sort of example that student would accept as an unselfish act, or what the student thinks it means to say that an act or person was unselfish. (Paul 1993, 336)

The discussion generated by these questions should explore the concepts of selfish or unselfish behavior, the kinds of examples that illustrate selfishness or, conversely, unselfishness. And finally, and perhaps most importantly, such a discussion will examine what kinds of assumptions we make when we state ideas in such general terms.

Socratic discussion places a great responsibility on both participants and the moderator. To take part effectively, one has to listen carefully for the reasons given, recognize underlying assumptions, discover the implications, and seek to find analogies, examples, and contrary evidence. The teacher quoted earlier in this chapter used Socratic questions as she probed for reasons that students might give for their estimation of the protagonist's age.

By becoming familiar with generic Socratic questions, teachers can seize the moment and build on students' natural interests. Examples of such questions are:

What do you mean by . . . ?
Could you put that another way?
Could you give me another example?
Is this always the case? What variables might change it?
What assumption underlies this thought?
Are these reasons adequate?
What is an alternative?
What effect would that have?
How can we find out more information?

Socratic questioning can probe students' thinking on a variety of issues. These discussions can occur at the beginning, middle, or end of an assignment. For instance, before reading *Julius Caesar* a Socratic discussion could explore the concepts of loyalty, power, and the role of government. During the reading, Socratic questioning could probe the motivation of Cassius, Brutus, and Mark Antony. Finally, as a review, Socratic questioning could return to the initial topics and apply them to any of the characters in the drama.

What is really called for in Socratic questioning is a determined exploration of a subject. Probing an issue in depth requires clarification, analysis, and evaluation. Socratic questioning is admirably suited for these processes. If a class were involved in a study of *Tess of the D'Urbervilles*, for instance, its members could look at Tess' behavior to determine the causative factors from both literary and psychological perspectives. While Socratic questions can spontaneously evolve in relation to student responses, the following list suggests a way to probe this topic.

*Sample Socratic Questions*

1. What instances in the novel indicate that Tess has arrived at some degree of self understanding?
2. Explain how these instances contributed to her deeper knowledge of self.
3. To what degree does this self-knowledge affect her subsequent actions?
4. What evidence suggests that Tess has developed significant insights about her personality?
5. To what degree is her self-knowledge influenced by her circumstances or society?
6. How is Tess' behavior consistent with her self perception, or how is it not?
7. How does her self-knowledge contrast to others' perception of her?
8. What irony, if any, might be related to Tess' understanding of herself?
9. What evidence is most significant as you determine her arriving at self-knowledge?
10. How does Tess' awareness of self contribute to the novel's conflict?
11. Which instance of self awareness is the most critical to Tess' overall development? Why?
12. How does Tess' reaction to Angel reflect this her knowledge of self? To Alec?

Socratic questioning is also a way to develop ideas in composition. Students can investigate their understandings of a topic through asking a series of questions as an effort to investigate all its major aspects.

A moderator's goals remain the same whether the leader is the teacher or a student. The moderator questions strategically to delve more deeply into a subject. She or he ensures that responses to answers maintain an investigative mode. Neither teachers nor students should lapse into monologues or lectures.

## Evaluation of Seminar Discussion

Of special concern to teachers embarking on seminar discussions is that this method of instruction threatens our instructional planning. We can no longer expect to control outcomes. We have to be willing to value exploration over correct answers. One of my journal entries considers this problem:

> I am not concerned about correctness nor completeness, but the working on a process—a stretching, if you will—an expanding of strategies. If these activities foster certain strategies that can lead to more "intuitive" thinking—increased problem solving—and eventually right or better answers—or even more confidence, then they have a worth, intrinsically. It has been our concern for "rightness" that has limited our classroom techniques to lecture/responses. Divergent thinking is not encouraged because it is often wrong. If I place a value on correctness of answers, rather than on the struggle for understanding, I am delimiting learning.

During a discussion, it is difficult to determine what type of thinking is going on. On the other hand, by listening to audiotapes afterwards it is possible to detect trends, commonalities, and changes. I collected tapes from one twelfth grade class over the course of a year and discovered some interesting behaviors. I was, first of all, genuinely pleased with the quality of the discussions. My journal entry reflects those thoughts:

> If the last tapes were more probing, the first tapes contained many excellent examples of analysis. Particularly well done was the delving into the personality of Emelia as contrasted to Othello. They discussed whether Emelia's turning against her husband was a change in personality. The class decided her personality did not change. Her characteristic of loyalty remained constant; she merely shifted her loyalty from her husband to Desdemona. Othello, on the other hand, they felt did change. He lost his nobility of character by his act of violence against Desdemona.

A striking aspect of the discussions was the equitable distribution of speaking time. Partly this was because of the design of the assignments, following the guidelines described earlier. Beyond the structure, though, it also seemed that the individuals were really listening to each other. In addition, when I studied a semester's collection of small group and whole class discussion tapes, I found seven distinctive trends that indicated thinking and learning were probably taking place.

1. More people became involved in whole class discussions as the semester progressed. Responses were shorter and students interacted more.
2. Students generated more questions. There was less willingness to accept statements without challenging them.
3. Contrary views were presented with evidence for justification more frequently. Students made "because-statements."
4. With increasing challenges to statements, students tried to work out the contrary views as well as their own opinions so that they could refute opposition or explain their own position better.
5. Students appeared more willing to take risks by making tentative statements, or asking questions. These behaviors were present in the small group discussions from the start, but by the end of the study they were showing up in the whole class discussions, too.
6. My teacher role diminished. My voice is quite apparent on the early tapes, asking questions or responding to student questions. During a later discussion, a student asks me a question and three people intervene with answers.
7. More trust and respect are evident. Students encourage each other to respond.

Individual students also seemed to change in their learning styles. The most striking contrast was between Ginny's and Beth's later performances compared to their earlier ones. Ginny had been reluctant to speak out in whole class discussions except when her group members were the presenters. During the *Wuthering Heights* discussion held near the end of the semester, Ginny initiated responses on several occasions. Beth, on the other hand, moved in a different direction. Beth, never a reluctant participant, made pronouncement-type statements in early discussions that had the effect of closing dialogue. On the *Wuthering Heights* tape, however, after a brief tentative speculation about risk to which Jan replies, "You can trust us," Beth does, indeed, take a giant risk by asking a question that had been bothering her:

> Well, you know, about being influenced by his [Heathcliff's] environment, the one thing I sort of didn't understand in the book was, your childhood is, like, the biggest part, the most important time, when you're really being influenced and, um, and Mr. Earnshaw really loved him, and, like, Catherine really loved him and everything like that, why—how come that didn't have as much effect on him when things did change and when Hindley was all mean to him?

Beth's question sparked a lively discussion with several responses. "Perhaps Mr. Earnshaw died too soon." "Maybe it was because Heathcliff's quiet and shy nature led him to need Mr. Earnshaw's protection. When that was removed, he decided to take revenge." Beth had risked appearing foolish and had been accepted by her classmates.

## Exploratory Speech, Seminar Discussion, and Critical Thinking

Trying to prove a definitive connection between exploratory speech, seminar discussion, and critical thinking is not yet possible with our current tools. For instance, it is difficult to show to what extent writing or speaking generated new understandings. Although some educators may claim that teachers can achieve predictable results from certain strategies, too many variables exist in the learning environment. We are not sure what knowledge or experience preexisted, for instance. Nor do we know what other events coincide with the classroom activities. It seems, however, we can mark trends such as the ones described above. These behaviors, if we determine them to be evidence of thoughtfulness, are recordable and observable. The kinds of attitudes that they indicate are marks of an inquiring mind and a willingness to collaborate. Instead of being satisfied with being "right," these students gained an appetite for inquiry into literature meanings. Seminar discussions and exploratory speech, if practiced regularly, have that kind of potential for all students.

*Teacher-Researcher Questions*

1. If students assume reponsibility for speech acts in whole class discussion, how might they achieve more understanding of a literary text?
2. How can the role of discussion moderator become part of the instructional process?
3. To what extent can students' writing or speaking activities demonstrate their ability to build concepts?
4. What kinds of behavioral trends might be revealed if transcripts of class discussions were collected for a period of time?

# • *ACTIVITIES* •

## CREATIVE QUESTION RESPONSE

OBJECTIVE: Students learn to understand the literature through probing for meaning in different forms of writing and discussion.

PROCESS:

1. After reading a work of literature, give students an open question to answer about a character, situation, setting, or theme. Their response can be in the form of paragraphs, a script, or free verse.
2. Students meet in small groups to share their writings. A recorder lists the most interesting, provocative, and significant ideas or approaches to the question.
3. These ideas are written on large sheets of newsprint with magic markers.

4. Small groups take turns in the front of the room explaining their ideas. If scripts or poetry were written, the groups can read or perform them for the class.
5. Following the presentations, the whole class discusses the ideas, looking for contrasting views and new insights.
6. Students revise their writings based on any new information or perspectives gained.

WHY THIS WORKS: Students not only recall major events of the literature, but on another level they are called upon to interpret these events. The second level of learning is assimilative, connecting the fragments into a more unified whole.

*Example*

OPEN QUESTION: Imagine you are Lady Macbeth. Imagine Lady Macbeth appears in Act 4 in a prominent role. How would you behave, as Lady Macbeth? Why?

(In preparation for this assignment, I wrote a sample journal and script. My writing aids in lesson planning and helps me experience the kinds of learning that might take place.)

### Journal

Lady Macbeth cannot appear mad as Macbeth does. Her signs of mental imbalance would have to be subtle—a withdrawn, less exuberant personality, and perhaps a lack of desire to eat, or particularly sleep, which fits the theme and her later behavior in Act Five. Her conversations would be with the gentlewoman or servants. Their behavior would be less respectful toward her, indicating her loss of stature in the court.

Perhaps she would call a servant to send a message to Lady Macduff, but he would refuse, having a more pressing demand from the king. This might be the second message she gives the servant; the first was a request for Macbeth to come to her chamber. Macbeth, we would learn, was not able to come because of his preparation for war. The advantage of adding this scene might have increased the poignancy of the slaughter of Lady Macduff and her children. Or an element of chance could be introduced, similar to that in *Romeo and Juliet*. The first message she sends to Lady Macduff does not actually go, but it is sidetracked by Macbeth, and the second one is dispatched too late to be effective.

*Script*

Lady Macbeth, when the servant reappears with a message that
Macbeth cannot attend her, is startled.

LADY MACBETH: What for! Are you not on the mission I directed?
SERVANT: Your Royal Head has placed an order on my hands.
The haste of military preparation o'ercomes all domestic banali-
ties.
LADY MACBETH: What hour is it?
SERVANT: It is the eleventh hour, Madam. (Exit)
LADY MACBETH: I see the candlelight creates shadows on the
walls, as images of children's fantasies. A crown that fits a
woman's head without the sword a man will bear. I see the dagger,
small, fitted with jewels, just for a woman's hand. But note how
it melts and disappears when I touch it. Just so, is the control
within my hands, only a picture shadow. The stuff of dreams.

## INANIMATE OBJECTS

OBJECTIVE: Students learn to appreciate how authors use
objects to create meanings through metaphorical connections.

PROCESS:

1. After reading a work of fiction, or during the reading, ask
   students to find three inanimate objects mentioned in the
   text. They should note the page and the reference. They
   write a journal describing each object and its significance to
   the plot, meaning, theme, or character.
2. Students form a large circle and share their objects, descriptions, and meanings with the class, in turn. Each person
   talks about only one of the objects in their list. If the same
   objects have been selected, students should still explain
   their own personal interpretation of meanings.
3. A recorder lists the objects and meanings either on newsprint or the chalkboard.
4. After all objects and meanings have been shared, students
   can discuss the relative merits of each and look for connections to other aspects of the story.

5. The teacher can act as moderator of this discussion or appoint student leaders.
6. The recorder or an appointed summarizer can present the major findings.
7. Follow up with a writing activity. Students can either write an analytical essay about the relative importance of one inanimate object in the text, or write a free verse from the point of view of that object about some aspect of the plot, characters, or events.
8. Alternative: Students can create a poster collage of the inanimate objects. These will provide visual imagery to enhance the learning climate.

WHY THIS WORKS: Students have a choice in selecting an object and deciding its meaning. The diversity of choices and interpretations increases literary understanding and allows students to practice explaining meanings to their peers. Answers are neither "right" nor "wrong"; they merely represent differing views. This lesson also yields a discussion of metaphors and their value in our understanding of events.

*Examples*
> From *Ethan Frome*: The pickle dish, the sled, the tree
> From *Macbeth*: The dagger, Macbeth's letter to Lady Macbeth, the empty chair at the banquet table
> From *Romeo and Juliet*: Romeo's mask, the balcony, the vial of poison

Since any objects mentioned in text are conceived of by the author as part of the work, it makes little difference what students select.

## OPPOSING SIDES

OBJECTIVE: Students learn to develop and answer challenging questions as a way to explore deeper meanings.

PROCESS:

1. After reading a work of literature, or while in process, each student generates three questions about the plot, character motivation, and/or theme.
2. Divide the class in half. Each half shares their questions to make a master list. As they share their questions, they rank them in order, easiest to hardest.
3. Select one student as moderator.
4. Side A sits facing Side B in two semi-circles. The moderator sits between the ends of each group. Everyone should have eye contact. The moderator calls on Side A to ask a question; Side B has one minute to answer the question. After one minute, Side A has one minute to expand on B's answer or challenge them. Side B then asks Side A a question and the pattern continues with the moderator timing and keeping control.
5. The moderator provides closure by summarizing major ideas.
6. Follow up with writing. Students select one of their own or the opposite side's questions. For homework they write the question and compose an answer including the class's ideas and their own conclusions.

WHY THIS WORKS: Students rephrase the literature in their own words. This activity is an opportunity to clarify confusing elements about a story. It is also an opportunity to practice leadership roles and active listening skills, and to participate in an open discussion setting where they have selected the topics. Students, for instance, used this method to clarify some of the puzzles in Conrad's story *The Secret Sharer* as they probed the guilt or innocence of the captain. The values and the morality inherent in such dramatic situations make good topics for discussion. Students in these exchanges tend to elaborate on ideas and to relate events to their own lives, thus "owning" the literature experience more.

## DISCUSSION PROMPTS

OBJECTIVE: Students become familiar with elements of story development as they practice elaborating on themes, setting, and characterization.

PROCESS:

1. After reading a literary work, divide the class into four groups. Give each group a problem to explore with an informal writing.

   a. Select a character and explain the influence of heredity and environment on the development of that character's personality.

   b. Analyze the use of setting in this novel and its purpose in developing the plot, theme, and/or an individual character's personality.

   c. Analyze the author's most significant message about life and describe how this message is developed through character interaction and setting.

   d. Analyze the development of a relationship between any two characters in this text and explain the major contributing factors in this development.

2. Students meet in small groups and share ideas. They choose the three most important ideas from their collection and rank these with the most important first.

3. Form a whole class circle with groups sitting together. The teacher is the moderator, or selected students from each group. Students are given sheets with all four statements and space to write notes about answers.

4. Group A presents their most important idea. Class members ask questions to clarify. Group B presents their most important idea and class members ask questions, and so on.

5. If time remains, repeat the process with each group's second idea.

6. A representative of each group summarizes their major ideas.

7. Follow up with writing. Students are responsible for writing a substantive paragraph in response to each of the four problems.

WHY THIS WORKS: This activity encourages students to look beyond a plot summary approach to literature. They are led into the problematical area of why certain things occur and their possible meaning. The very broadness of the problems indicates an open response, but they also demand some kind of "proof" from the text itself. Again because the answers are neither Yes nor No, students are given the freedom to explore possible meanings. That kind of risk taking enlarges perspectives. Since students have a responsibility for a follow-up writing, they also become more active listeners to the other groups' presentations.

# ● Five
. . . . . . . . . . . . . . . . . .

## Cooperative Learning and Small Groups

> Within cooperative learning groups there is a process of interpersonal exchange that promotes the use of higher-level thinking strategies, higher-level reasoning, and metacognitive strategies. — *Johnson and Johnson*

*A* thinking class usually turns to cooperative learning and small groups as part of its process. The trouble with small groups is that they are unpredictable. On the one hand, they can be dynamic combinations producing the greatest results a teacher could imagine. On the other hand, they can be pedestrian, limited in outlook, and unimaginative. Both kinds can exist in the same classroom—on the same day. Those who claim unrestricted benefits from small groups have not lived with them in a 30' × 30' room day after day, through the first snowfall, homecoming dances, and the annual magazine drive—year after year. Accepting the fact that they can fail is essential to progress. Understanding that they need not fail is essential, too.

Although group work has many benefits, it is different from individual work. It is slow and cumbersome, lacking the efficiency of a single person's effort. It has been noted that groups spend an average of fifty-eight seconds on a topic. They tend to jump from subject to subject. The reason that superior thinking is generated by groups is that collectively they possess more information than does any one individual. This depth and diversity allow the analytic abilities of a group to surpass that of an individual. We call the result the "assembly effect."

This effect is the reason why in a democracy we rely on juries, Congress, and the Supreme Court (Fisher 1974).

We hear so many comments about small groups, both negative and positive, that it is hard to sort out the truth from the myths. These myths imply either that small groups are some sort of magic panacea for all the ills of current educational problems or that they are a colossal time waster. The truth about small groups is that they *can* work. *Making* them work takes time, patience, coordination, and some knowledge about communication on the part of the teacher as well as lots of practice by the students.

## Seven Myths

We will look at seven myths about communication and small groups in an effort to better understand some of the major pitfalls they represent.

Myth 1: *All students have the communication skills necessary to work effectively in small groups.*

While we were all born with an innate ability for language and we all possess the need to communicate, we are not inherently adept in the communication skills needed to work in small groups. Simply placing people into groups does not magically transform those individuals into proficient group members. Interpersonal and group processing skills are learned behaviors. Omitting this kind of instruction jeopardizes small group effectiveness (Johnson and Johnson 1989–1990).

Myth 2: *Teaching communication skills will help all students to interact successfully in small groups.*

While learning about communication and its skills can improve interaction in most situations, it is not a cure-all. Communication cannot be improved by simply learning some skills. The "rules" for communication are not infallible. "If such rules were available, they could be printed and distributed at freshman orientation and all departments of

English and Speech Communication could be disbanded" (King 1988, 256). Improving communication is a complex, lifelong process.

So many variables exist in any communication event that outcomes are not universally similar. One participant may have a headache, another might be anticipating a vacation, the terminology might be unfamiliar to another, and the material may seem irrelevant to still others. Any and all of these conditions preclude each group member from receiving the same messages as do the others. Communication is a receiver phenomenon. While the speaker might follow the "rules" for success, ultimately the communication process is not complete until the receiver has processed the message and gleaned its meaning.

Myth 3: *The best way to improve communication is to become a better speaker.*

Listening is more important than speaking if we want to improve our communication. More than 50 percent of communication depends upon our ability to listen. Listening, in fact, may be our most important communication skill. First of all, we spend 42 to 57 percent of our communication time listening (Cooper 1991). Listening is the way we establish and maintain our interpersonal relationships. We listen to identify and interpret messages, and our accuracy determines our health, well-being, and success in social and work situations. Yet listening is the least taught communication skill, and speech the next to least taught.

Different authors categorize the types of listening we engage in, but basically there are four: appreciative, informative, evaluative, and empathic.

1. Appreciative: Listening for the pleasure of sounds or the experience—to the laughter of children or a symphony by Beethoven.
2. Informative: Listening for specific data—for the weather report or directions to a friend's house.

3. Evaluative: Listening to determine the worth or accuracy of information—to an insurance policy's benefits or a political candidate's promise.
4. Empathic: Listening to experience the feelings of others— to a client's complaint or a child's story.

The lines between these forms are thin. We may use some evaluative listening when we are receiving information. We may listen to poetry appreciatively and then informatively as we determine the message. Empathic listening is especially difficult, but most valuable when we want to build relationships and truly communicate well.

Myth 4: *Small group socializing is a waste of time.*

Small groups need to build a comfortable climate in order to be productive. Teachers often observe that students talk enough already and that in small groups, they spend too much time socializing. However, we should consider the social norms in any conversation. We generally don't begin with business. People need some time to adjust to each other and the context of the conversation. Socializing, rather than being counterproductive, actually reduces tensions. If those primary tensions are not diminished, the work of the group probably will not be satisfactory. Consider our adult work groups. People chat about inconsequential matters as they get to know each other in a new situation. Even longtime friends alternate between personal and business matters. Teachers should not view students' socializing with alarm, because it is a natural element in our lives. Furthermore, these social interchanges actually help the work of the group.

Taking the time to build a social climate improves openness and the exchange of ideas. If we are talking to friends, we will take more risks and share our thoughts more easily. Building a feeling of cohesion is important for building trust.

Myth 5: *Successful small groups are conflict free.*

Conflict in small groups is inevitable for several reasons. It begins with the primary tension people feel as they begin to work in groups. Five people meeting together will naturally have different tastes, experiences, and knowledge. At first this discomfort is hidden as people politely conceal their views. If the group never moves beyond this courteous concealment, the group will not achieve success. Why? Because they will not freely express their thoughts and they will lose the creative impulse needed for synergy, or the power that emerges as a combined result of their efforts. Instead, they will be struggling with their emotional needs rather than releasing energy for the task.

Groupthink, when all agree without protest despite contrary knowledge, can be dangerous. The failed Bay of Pigs invasion during the John F. Kennedy administration is a classic case. President Kennedy's small group of advisors did not conduct a rational and systematic examination of the evidence available at the time. "No one wanted to appear to lack confidence in the information or the training, so there were no comments critical of the plan, which turned out to be total disaster" (Zeuschner 1993, 199). People must talk, argue, compare, and suggest. New ideas disturb the peace. However, original thoughts emerge from this process. When groups truly cooperate, ideas proposed by individuals become incorporated into a joint effort. Suggestions are not simply accepted or turned down, they are molded to fit new concepts.

Myth 6: *Majority rule is the best way to make decisions.*

Being raised in a democracy leads us to think that majority rule is the best way to make decisions in a small group. This method may make sense for a nation, but in a small group it has serious disadvantages. The minority lose their commitment to carry out the task. Even the majority may have different reasons for their choice, so the possibility for dissension is extreme. Majority rule creates polarization, dissatisfaction, and resentment. Thus decisions by majority vote can be thought of as win-lose choices.

Compromise is another frequent procedure for making decisions. It, too, has severe problems. For one, the decision may be a poor one, based as it is on no one's best idea, but pieces of several. We can think of compromise as a lose-lose decision. No one gets what she or he wants; thus, no one may feel particularly committed to the project.

The best decision-making process is consensus. It is the most difficult and time consuming way to decide, but this technique is worth the cost, for it results in a win-win situation. Increased productivity, member satisfaction, and commitment to the task are all benefits from consensus.

Practicing consensus-making helps to make it more workable and natural. Accepting the benefits of win-win solutions over their procedural drawbacks requires familiarity with the give and take of talking ideas through. Many of the activities in this book can become opportunities for work on consensus. The shortcuts of majority rule or compromise, so commonly resorted to, will become less desirable once students have experienced the satisfaction of talking problems through to consensus.

Myth 7: *Small groups eliminate shyness.*

Small groups are not a guarantee that shyness will disappear. People working together in small groups tend to be more confident speakers than when faced with larger gatherings. There is less formality and more opportunity to express opinions in a small group setting. But people with high communication apprehension (CA), or fear of speaking in public, may be equally apprehensive in a small group. Unfortunately, this fact is little recognized, and classrooms do not prepare students to cope with these problems.

Extremely shy people are often perceived negatively in small groups. They exhibit one of the so-called dysfunctional behaviors on the lists of small group dos and don'ts: withdrawal. As teachers and peers we may catch ourselves saying to these individuals, "If you wanted to speak, you would." And yet it is seldom that simple. When we monitor group behavior we may find these students are consistently silent. And they may display other behaviors we regard as dysfunctional, as well. Highly apprehensive people tend to pause longer than the average person, and are more inclined to use filler expressions, such as "you know." Their remarks may be irrelevant to the topic, but most significantly, they will avoid disagreement in small groups (McCroskey and Richmond 1988).

Since these behaviors inhibit the progress of the group, and are viewed negatively by other members, the individual experiences increased discomfort. Speech and thought are connected; therefore, as the communication flow is blocked in these people, so are their thoughts. If they were working alone, they could generate ideas. Within a group, their thoughts are frozen, and they contribute less of substance than other group members.

Helping all students increase their awareness of communication apprehension, its effects and its antidotes, should become an integral part of communication instruction. One possibility is for students to take a self-test and score their reactions. McCroskey and Richmond (1991) have developed one, the Personal Report of Communication Apprehension-24 (PRCA-24), which appears in the Activity section of this chapter. The PRCA-24 determines one's sense of discomfort in different situations: groups, meetings, interpersonal relations, and public address. People with high CA are uncomfortable in all of those places; those with average scores usually show discomfort in one or more. In other words, this survey affords insights on behavior for both the children and the teacher.

## Cooperative Learning Strategies

Despite the myths about small group process, and despite the problems, the literature abounds with stories of its success (Brilhart and Galanes 1989). The findings of research on cooperative learning are generally positive. Group work produces more actively engaged, task-oriented behavior than when students work alone on "seatwork." The struggling student profits from an interactive situation where she or he receives feedback from peers. And, students at all achievement levels benefit from the opportunity to "rehearse" new concepts as they talk through problems.

Social cooperation increases as students learn more about each other. They reveal their achievements—hang gliding, clown therapy, Army Reserve training, and motherhood. Students also admit their vulnerabilities—dropping out of football, failing typing, not winning a debate tournament, and losing parents through death or divorce. That kind of information may not seem relevant to language arts, but those same human experiences are ultimately the stuff of any literary text.

## Improving Listening Behaviors

Improving our relations with others really begins with listening. Listening for all four purposes, appreciation, information, evaluation, and empathy, can be improved through nonverbal as well as verbal behavior. When our bodies are attuned to the speakers, we are more open to their message. As listeners we should strive for good listening behavior by:

Maintaining natural eye contact
Nodding the head in agreement
Leaning forward
Adopting a pleasant facial expression
Facing the speaker(s)
Keeping arms open (not folded)
Taking a position at the same elevation as the speaker

If these nonverbal behaviors are choreographed for effect without sincerity, they will have the opposite effect. People have an uncanny ability to detect nonverbal behavior that is inconsistent with the person or the message. Others will detect our deception and our credibility will drop. And our gestures and facial expressions can double-cross us even when we are sincere. We may, for example, avoid looking at people or turn to one side when they speak. Knowing that these behaviors send a negative message helps us to change. For that reason, students should understand the importance of nonverbal "talk."

When groups are formed everyone should sit, preferably in a circle, so they have eye contact with everyone else. They should learn to give nonverbal signals, such as nodding or smiling, to indicate they are attentive. If the situation calls for it, they should take notes. This kind of nonverbal behavior helps them to avoid listening distractions and signals their interest to the speakers.

Active listening requires conscious effort. The behaviors and skills of listening are teachable and can become part of the instructional program. The following list of suggestions can help to model classroom listening instruction:

*Suggestions for Improving Listening*

1. *Be prepared.* In order to listen well we must be physically and mentally ready. We should choose to sit in a place where we can hear. If necessary, have pen and paper ready for note taking. Our minds should be set in anticipation for the topic. We will have read any material that is to be discussed.

2. *Set Goals.* We need to establish a purpose for listening, plan how we will use the information we hear, and find motivation factors in the message.

3. *Use Time Effectively.* We have to utilize the gap in time between the average speaker's rate (approximately 150 words per minute) and the average thinking rate (approximately 400 words per minute). Since we think approximately three or more times faster than we can speak, we process messages more rapidly than a speaker sends us his words. Thus we tend to fill that space with distracting thoughts, reducing our concentration on the speaker's message. Research indicates that when messages are delivered at a faster rate, 190 or more words per minute, they are more easily comprehended and believed. This improvement is probably because the shorter time gap inten-

sifies the listener's effort (Wolff, Marsnick, Tacey, and Nichols 1983).

Our strategy should be to use the thinking space productively: to take notes, write questions, study verbal and nonverbal cues, review mentally, reorder information, and find patterns.

4. *Minimize Distractions.* We need to control emotional reactions. When emotions turn on, the intellect turns off unless we are aware of what triggers our response. For example, some words can send our blood pressure soaring: "Nazi," "gay rights," or "feminism." Some individuals' behaviors or appearance can spark anger or fear: kids with dreadlocks, opaque sunglasses, loud voices, or street language.

We also need to avoid developing counterarguments. Concentrating on what *we* will say next, we lose the speaker's message.

We should avoid evaluation as much as possible. Non-evaluative listening precludes saying, "That's a dumb idea" or "That'll never work." Words like these shut down ideas and shut down minds.

There is a place for evaluative response, of course. When someone makes a questionable claim, it's appropriate to ask where he or she found the information. Requesting support for conclusions is part of critical thinking. Making those requests in a tone of inquiry rather than challenge forestalls defensiveness. But evaluation should be the last part of the listening process, not the first.

5. *Use Feedback.* Feedback is the only way the speaker knows the message was received. Feedback can be nonverbal: nods, smiles, laughter. Verbal feedback clarifies messages: asking questions, paraphrasing, affirming responses (okay, yes), negative responses (no, maybe), and asking for clarifications. Example:

"When you said you didn't want to go to the Francks' on Saturday night, I understood that to mean you don't want to socialize with them."

"No, I like the Francks. It's just that I have to work all weekend preparing that year-end report. I'm really uptight about it, and I just wouldn't enjoy myself."

## Small Group Composition

Much debate centers around the way groups are constructed. Should students choose their groups? Should the teacher assign groups? If so, how?

Part of that debate involves grouping by ability, either heterogeneous or homogeneous. Research is mixed about which grouping is better. Many scholars claim that heterogeneous grouping works well for any ability level. Other studies show high-ability students doing better in homogeneous groups (Cohen and Benton 1988). The contradictory results for high academic achievers in the different groupings may well rest more on their communication training than on their ability level.

Research findings, on the other hand, consistently show that lower-ability students benefit more from heterogeneous than from homogeneous groupings. Receiving explanations from peers not only improves their understanding, but also cues them into the processes of asking questions and knowing how to find answers. In addition, certain types of students appear to benefit more than others. Black students, and possibly Hispanic, apparently profit even more from cooperative learning experiences than do Anglo students (Good and Brophy 1991).

When grouping students, it is most important to consider reluctance to communicate, especially when the projects are long term. Since grouping to overcome fear is not dealt with in any literature as yet, I shall describe that process.

After explaining that the best work depends on full participation from each person, and that reluctance to speak is a normal reaction in some situations, I set up small groups by scores on the PRCA-24 self-assessment test. Into each group I place one person with a high apprehension score, one with a low score, and the rest with average levels. Students typically tell me that this method leads to their best-ever group experience. One student called it "magic." Their work reflects this enthusiasm. I think there are two reasons. First, talking frankly and openly about the problem of communication fear acknowledges that it is a more common condition than they had previously thought. Second, students realize that their responsibility as participants in a group involves listening supportively to others and not just speaking brilliantly. When they perceive that success means facilitating group discussion, not dominating it, they can relax and help each other achieve a win-win situation. The highly fearful feel less uncomfortable, and if they are quiet, the group members understand that it is not because they are snobs or unfriendly.

Another grouping method I have found effective is based on sociograms. They have several advantages. If multiple topics of study are offered, students select three that interest them. They also write names of three people they want to work with, and I guarantee they will get one topic of choice or one person of choice. Usually, I can give students a topic and at least one person from their lists. This method operates well because students have some say in what they will be doing, and someone with whom they like to work. The matching and setting up for the groups consumes several hours, so that time should be programmed into the preparation.

Grouping can also be spontaneous choice. If part of the training in small groups is to get along with others socially, and if a classroom climate improves as students get to know each other better, then it is beneficial to the group in different ways. When small groups are needed for buzz sessions, brainstorming, or one-class-period projects, it is reasonable to simply count off into groups. Another easy way is to have students pair off for responding, devising questions, or preplanning activities. Working in twos, or dyads, has the advantage of guaranteeing that each person will be talking almost 50 percent of the time. Dyads, because they are less threatening to those who are reluctant communicators, are a good intermediate step to small groups.

Forming small groups is a natural progression. Two pairs join to make groups of four. If the number of pairs is uneven, one group can have six members, even though groups larger than five seem to be less productive. Teachers who have not used small groups before find this pairing method a comfortable way to introduce grouping. Neither teachers nor students are placed in vulnerable positions.

## Small Group Training

Working in classroom small groups is not a "natural" arrangement. In our personal lives we do not choose to work closely with strangers. We seek out folks with similar likes and interests. The effort of communicating with unfamiliar people creates stress and requires new skills. Students have to learn behaviors that foster cooperation and diminish distrust. New norms have to be learned, practiced, and internalized. Probably most experiments with small groups fail because the training part of the project was omitted. Many teachers assume that once students are in small groups, the work will progress as it does in the whole class. The difference is that in a whole class setting, the work goes on under the teacher's direct supervision. In the small groups, students have to be self-directed, and that kind of behavior requires skillful planning and monitoring.

Some preliminary activities encourage social talk and build group identity. One idea is for the groups to decide on a name and a logo. Part of choosing the name and designing the logo is to make sure that they represent the talents and interests of the group. Or, groups can design shields with each section representing something special about a group member. After these activities, the groups present their products to the class and explain *why* they chose as they did. Establishing these social bonds speeds later work because it relaxes defensive behaviors and overcomes listening barriers.

Group work should be planned to achieve clear objectives, even in the preliminary stages. A loose structure invites procrastination and wasted time. Three essential guidelines aid this structure, in addition to having students pre-prepare a product for sharing.

1. *Establish a time limit and stick to it.* A fifteen-minute segment is usually sufficient for in-class group work. Some groups will be finished in five, and some will need all day. If they quickly complete the task, ask them to repeat the steps to be sure nothing was forgotten, or ask them to explain what they have done. For those who have not finished in the time limit, see if one more minute will help. That additional minute can be granted, but start to move back to whole class discussion. Knowing that time limits are honored promotes on-task behavior.

2. *Assign specific tasks.* Groups unsure of what is expected will waste time and energy. Review their responsibilities before they break into groups. If clear instructions are given prior to forming groups, the students can focus on the task more completely without being distracted unduly by the demands of social interaction.

3. *Require a product.* At the end of the time, students will have prepared a list, made an outline, selected phrases, chosen a reading, constructed questions, assigned readers, or found an answer.

As group work begins in a class, these guidelines are essential. Once students are accustomed to the self-direction of group work or projects are well under way, the students can revise these guidelines to serve their own purpose. One other technique that I have found helpful is to assign points for completion of procedural tasks. This kind of extrinsic motivation, however small, increases motivation.

## Functional Roles

Social scientists have determined that if a group is to be successful certain functional roles must come into play. These roles fall into two categories: task and maintenance. Task roles are significant because they help the group complete its assignment. Maintenance roles are also vital because they help the group to build their social relationships. The ideal ratio between task and maintenance roles is two to one, with task roles occurring twice as often as social ones.

The most necessary task role is Information Giver. If the group lacks knowledge, its likelihood of success is minimal. With that in mind, teachers might be well advised to assure that each group has a member with strong abilities in that area. Likewise, groups often fail if they lack maintenance roles like Supporter or Harmonizer. Someone in the group should be able to say, "Good job. We really needed that help," or "John, what do you think about that idea?"

Handing out a list of "Small Group Task and Maintenance Roles and Behaviors" makes the expectations clear. Suggestions to help in role training can be found in the Activities section at the end of this chapter.

### Small Group Task and Maintenance Roles and Behaviors

| Task Role | Behaviors |
|---|---|
| 1. Initiator | Contributes ideas and suggestions |
| 2. Information Seeker | Asks for clarification, relevant information |
| 3. Information Giver | Offers facts or examples |
| 4. Opinion Seeker | Asks for contributions of ideas |
| 5. Opinion Giver | States beliefs or opinions |
| 6. Elaborator | Builds on others' ideas with examples or hypotheses |
| 7. Summarizer | Pulls ideas together, suggests an integration of information |
| 8. Procedure Developer | Handles routine tasks, arranges seating |
| 9. Recorder | Keeps notes on the group's progress |

| | |
|---|---|
| 10. Evaluator | Analyzes group's work and checks progress |

| *Maintenance Roles* | *Behaviors* |
|---|---|
| 1. Supporter | Praises, agrees with, and accepts contributions of others |
| 2. Harmonizer | Reconciles disagreements, seeks to reduce differences |
| 3. Tension Reliever | Relaxes the group through humor or informalities |
| 4. Gatekeeper | Keeps communication open, encourages silent members |
| 5. Feeling Expresser | Shares own feelings and expresses group's feelings |

(Adapted from Adler and Rodman 1991, 234–235)

Understanding these roles helps groups to function better. Practicing the roles helps even more. Individual members must be capable of fulfilling all of the functions. Overcoming tendencies to dominate or withdraw from conversations is only half the battle; students have to think about offering reassurance to their classmates and deliberately encouraging their comments.

The benefits to the students are greater than a better academic product. Just as practice in tennis improves the game, and one's confidence, so can small group discussions provide the support to raise one's confidence and self-concept. Shaowen, a member of a Small Group Communication class, describes these benefits:

> In my early childhood, I had the worst self-image. I could not look people in the eye when expressing myself. . . . My relationships are better now because there is communication on both sides. I find that relationships are much more gratifying if I am able to actually be a verbal part of them. Obtaining a better self-concept has not only helped in my relationships, but also in developing leadership skills that will benefit me in the future.

# *Classroom Research*

Most of the research regarding small group work in the classroom has been done by outside observers. Some of these researchers question whether the value of cooperative learning is sustainable year after year and if it is appropriate for all age groups or ability levels. Therefore, it would be valuable for the classroom teacher to also conduct research. Keeping journals about observations of behaviors, reactions, and effective methods can become an important part of the body of knowledge. Transcribing discussions and videotaping classroom activities are other ways to document results. We can monitor our own progress and diagnose our own mistakes. Students' comments, journals, and discussions are valuable data. The activities at the end of this chapter are intended to intensify the group process instruction and to encourage self-assessment by students. Any or all of the activities can become part of the teacher-researcher's data to document how effectively the process is working. Through methods such as these the real world of the classroom can bring fresh insights into the research.

So far, the theory supporting cooperative learning as a way to improve thinking is strong, but the practical application is a mixed story. Both teachers and students can stumble and fail without training in group process and discussion skills. Informing ourselves about these procedures and contributing information to our colleagues can improve our classroom interactions and benefit both our students and the profession.

*Teacher-Researcher Questions*
1. What kinds of groupings would help all students to participate more effectively?
2. To what extent might communication apprehension affect individual students' learning?
3. What methods might help students to assume more self-direction when they participate in small groups?
4. Which behaviors by individuals aid the most in achieving group satisfaction?

# • *ACTIVITIES* •

## COMMUNICATION APPREHENSION TEST (PRCA-24)

OBJECTIVE: This test is designed to measure communication apprehension (CA). Because many teachers, as well as students, have high levels of CA, they should determine their own feelings through this assessment. This test is suitable for students in grades seven and above.

PROCESS: Administer the Personal Report of Communication Apprehension-24 first to yourself and then to students.

*Personal Report of Communication Apprehension-24 (PRCA-24)*

Directions: This instrument is composed of twenty-four statements concerning feelings about communicating with other people. Please indicate the degree to which each statement applies to you by marking whether you (1) strongly agree, (2) agree, (3) are undecided, (4) disagree, or (5) strongly disagree. There are no right or wrong answers. Answer quickly; record your first impression.

1. I dislike participating in group discussions.
2. Generally, I am comfortable while participating in group discussions.
3. I am tense and nervous while participating in group discussions.
4. I like to get involved in group discussions.
5. Engaging in a group discussion with new people makes me tense and nervous.
6. I am calm and relaxed while participating in group discussions.
7. Generally, I am nervous when I have to participate in a meeting.
8. Usually, I am calm and relaxed when I am called upon to express an opinion at a meeting.
9. I am calm and relaxed when I am called upon to express an opinion at a meeting.
10. I am afraid to express myself at meetings.
11. Communicating at meetings usually makes me uncomfortable.

12. I am relaxed when answering questions at a meeting.
13. While participating in a conversation with a new acquaintance, I feel very nervous.
14. I have no fear of speaking up in conversations.
15. Ordinarily, I am very tense and nervous in conversations.
16. Ordinarily, I am very calm and relaxed in conversations.
17. While conversing with a new acquaintance, I feel very relaxed.
18. I'm afraid to speak in conversations.
19. I have no fear of giving a speech.
20. Certain parts of my body feel tense and rigid while giving a speech.
21. I feel relaxed while giving a speech.
22. My thoughts become confused and jumbled when I am giving a speech.
23. I face the prospect of giving a speech with confidence.
24. While giving a speech, I get so nervous I forget facts I really know.

## Scoring

The PRCA-24 permits computation of one total score and four subscores. The subscores are related to communication apprehension in each of four common communication contexts: group discussions, meetings, interpersonal conversations, and public speaking. To compute your scores, add or subtract your scores for each item as indicated below.

1. Group Discussions
   18 (plus) scores for items 2, 4, and 6; (minus) scores for items 1, 3, and 5.
   Subtotal:
2. Meetings
   18 (plus) scores for items 8, 9, and 12; (minus) scores for items 7, 10, and 11.
   Subtotal:
3. Interpersonal Conversations
   18 (plus) scores for items 14, 16, and 17; (minus) scores for items 13, 15, and 18.
   Subtotal:

4. Public Speaking

18 (plus) scores for items 19, 21, and 23; (minus) scores for items 20, 22, and 24.

Subtotal:

Grand Total:

Scores on the four contexts (groups, meetings, interpersonal conversations, and public speaking) can range from a low of 6 to a high of 30. Any score above 18 indicates some degree of apprehension. If your score is above 18 for the public speaking context, you are like the overwhelming majority of Americans.

### *Interpretation*

Any grand total score above 65 indicates that you are more generally apprehensive about communication than the average person. Scores above 80 indicate a very high level of communication apprehension. If your scores fall in the unusually high range (over 80), this may suggest that you will have some difficulty in implementing some of the suggestions made to help quiet students, because of your own fear of communication. Scores below 50 indicate a very low level of communication apprehension. If your score is quite low, you may have less tolerance than most teachers do for people who are fearful of communication. You may have to take extra care to understand the problems that the quiet child faces. Extreme scores (below 50 or above 80) are abnormal. This means that the degree of apprehension you experience may not be associated with a realistic response to a situation. For example, people with very low scores may not experience apprehension in situations in which they should, and people with very high scores might experience apprehension in situations where there is no rational reason for the anxiety.

About 20 percent of the population falls in each extreme category. People in the average range of communication apprehension tend to respond differently in different situations; for example, in a job-interview situation, they might be highly anxious, whereas in a familiar situation (e.g., teaching in their own classroom), they might experience no anxiety or tension at all. By contrast, both low and high communication-apprehensive people tend to respond to virtually all oral communication situations in their respective characteristic manners. This means that people with high communication apprehension tend to withdraw and remain quiet. An extreme score may indicate traitlike communication apprehension, an enduring orientation about communication that usually does not change unless there is some form of intervention. (McCroskey and Richmond, *Quiet Children and the Classroom Teacher*, 31–35. Copyright by the Speech Communication Association, 1991. Reprinted by permission of the publisher.)

WHY THIS WORKS: This relatively simple test has been validated with numerous subjects. It serves as an indication of the level of discomfort an individual feels and can guide instructional plans realistically.

## REACHING CONSENSUS

OBJECTIVE: Students experience the process of working toward consensus. Using a step-by-step method, students practice the skills of sharing information in order to arrive at a common product.

PROCESS:

1. Individuals generate ideas in response to a prompt; e.g., "List six phrases from the literary text that help to create the story's mood."
2. Ask individuals to rank the phrases in their effectiveness for creating mood, from least to best.
3. Divide the class into groups. Each member reads his or her list in the rank order, giving reasons for the top-placed phrase.
4. Combine the lists of all the members into one list.
5. Discuss and rank the top six. Use consensus to decide. Do not vote.
6. Assess the group's process. What problems emerged? What are the advantages and disadvantages of consensus in group decision making?

   Variation: Rank the phrases and their importance to the plot.

WHY THIS WORKS: The activity helps students to openly share ideas, and at the same time to probe more deeply into a text. The topic is not likely to engender high emotional responses as do some popular consensus activities involving values, such as choosing who should live or die.

## WRITER'S WORKSHOP

OBJECTIVE: Students participate in groups to share writings as a way to build knowledge and as preparation for revision.

PROCESS:

1. Students prepare writing assignments in advance of the workshop. These can be journal entries about on-going work, answering questions such as:
   a. What did you understand best?
   b. What is confusing about this lesson?
   c. How does this lesson compare to the previous one?

   Or assignments can be reports on field trips, interviews, research, laboratory experiments, or projects. Students may write monologues as if they were reporters viewing events in history, foreign countries, or in a literary text. Students may assume the persona of characters in fiction. They can describe characters, places, and events.

2. Day of the Workshop: Each student brings one writing he or she is willing to share. Divide the class into groups of four or five. The purpose of the group is to listen to the oral reading of the writings by the individuals and to respond constructively.

3. Person A reads his or her writing, and in turn B, C, D, and E tell A the answers to the following questions:
   a. What part was most interesting?
   b. What part would they like to know more about?
   c. What words, phrases, or descriptions did they like best?

4. After A's writing has been responded to, repeat the process with B, C, D, and E. Using this workshop throughout the year encourages both writing and speaking more effectively.

WHY THIS WORKS: Students practice sharing writings orally, which increases confidence in speaking interpersonally and aids writing skills. When we speak aloud we can hear how our words work to build ideas. Receiving feedback from peers, we can change and revise ideas to be more understandable.

## SMALL GROUP ROLES

OBJECTIVE: Students practice the different roles of task and maintenance functions in order to internalize their importance in successful small group operation.

PROCESS:

1. Explain the kinds of tasks and maintenance functions necessary for effective group process using the material in this chapter.
2. Hand out the following Task and Maintenance Chart.

*Task and Maintenance Chart*

| Roles | | | | Groups | |
|---|---|---|---|---|---|
| *Task* | 1 | 2 | 3 | 4 | 5 |
| 1. Initiator | | | | | |
| 2. Information-Seeker | | | | | |
| 3. Information-Giver | | | | | |
| 4. Opinion-Seeker | | | | | |
| 5. Opinion-Giver | | | | | |
| 6. Elaborator | | | | | |
| 7. Summarizer | | | | | |
| 8. Procedure-Developer | | | | | |
| 9. Recorder | | | | | |
| 10. Evaluator | | | | | |
| *Maintenance* | | | | | |
| 1. Supporter | | | | | |
| 2. Harmonizer | | | | | |
| 3. Tension-Reliever | | | | | |
| 4. Gatekeeper | | | | | |
| 5. Feeling-Expresser | | | | | |

3. Divide the class into groups of five.

4. Give each group an envelope with fifteen cards in it. Each card has a function written on it. Ten are task functions and five are maintenance functions. One member of the group hands out the cards at the beginning of the activity and collects them at the end. Each student will have two task cards and one maintenance card. If a group has less than five people, some individuals will have more than three function cards; if a group is larger than five, some will have fewer than three cards.

5. Hand out the case study given below. Students read and study the case for five minutes. At the end of that time, the groups discuss the case, trying to fulfill the roles on their cards. The discussion lasts ten minutes.

6. Form a large circle with the groups seated together. Circle five chairs in the center to form a "fishbowl."

7. Group 1 members take their place in the inner circle. While they discuss the case for five minutes, the class tallies the functions they observe in the Group 1 column. For instance, if someone initiates the discussion or presents a new idea, observers place a slash mark on the line by "Initiator" under column 1. If someone asks a question about facts, they place a slash mark on the line by "Information-Seeker" under column 1. After five minutes, stop Group 1. Discuss briefly what roles the observers noticed.

8. Continue the process with Groups 2 through 5, placing slash marks on the lines by the various functions in the appropriate column for that group, e.g., Column 2 for Group 2, etc.

9. After all of the groups have been through the process, the final discussion should cover what behaviors facilitated the groups' interaction most effectively. Avoid negative comments or redirect their focus. If, for example, students criticize quiet students, ask what functions by other members might have contributed to more equal participation. Next discuss the quality of the decisions reached.

<u>WHY THIS WORKS</u>: Students develop an awareness of the process of discussion and the pattern of interaction. Although students experience self-consciousness about their participation, especially in the fishbowl, they recognize the benefit of observing others. Limiting the fishbowl segments to five minutes diminishes the trauma. What they gain from this activity, however, is the knowledge that each individual plays a vital role in a discussion's success.

### The High School Alcohol Case

Your group has been appointed by the School Superintendent as a committee of students to study the High School Alcohol Case.

The Warren High School administration, disturbed by reports that groups of students have been drinking at team and organizational events, drew up a code of behavior that all students who wanted to participate in school activities had to sign. This code specified that if students were found to be drinking, they would be suspended from school for three days and lose their right to participate in school activities for three months.

Last Monday, an anonymous call to the principal, Mr. Casey, reported that members of the girls' field hockey team were present at a party in a local motel where alcohol was consumed. The party was Saturday night, and the field hockey team was not playing that weekend. Students from another district school, Manley High School, were also present.

Mr. Casey called the girls into his office, and they admitted they had been at the party. They also admitted that they had been drinking beer but denied that they were intoxicated. Their parents were informed, and the girls were suspended from school for three days and were not allowed to play field hockey for the rest of the season, as the behavior code specified.

The field hockey team is one of the best in the region and had been scheduled to compete in the playoffs in three weeks. They had been state champions the year before, and with the same starters on the team, hoped to claim a state championship again.

The parents of the girls protested the principal's decision, but Mr. Casey pointed out that he had the backing of the other administrators and the coaching staff, the girls were underage for drinking, and that they had willingly signed the code of behavior.

A letter to the editor of the *Lakeview Times*, the local paper, from a Manley High School student came to the girls' defense, citing that they had not violated the school's rules since it was a private party, not a school event, and that Manley High athletes had not been similarly punished. The letter has stirred up strong feelings in both school communities. Some parents from both schools are glad that Mr. Casey took the stand he did. Adolescents should not be drinking, and the schools should set the standard. Others feel that this kind of ruling unfairly targets one group of students when on any given weekend high school students are consuming beer at private parties with impunity.

The case has been sent to the Superintendent, Mrs. Coulter, as the uproar has increased. She has appointed a student committee comprised of one representative from each high school in the district to study the issue. She has informed the community she will follow the recommendations from your committee.

Your charge is to make a recommendation to the superintendent for a course of action.

## PAPER BAG PROJECT

OBJECTIVE: Students participate in an activity designed to provide an experience in group dynamics. The individual is expected to demonstrate cooperative behaviors in a problem-solving situation.

PROCESS: This is a two-day exercise in group building.

DAY ONE

1. Divide the class into groups of five. Give each group a shopping bag containing the following: newspapers, magic markers, streamers, balloons, construction paper, scissors, and tape. Tell the groups that their job is to decorate a section of the classroom. The project can be a representation of a theme or subject related to the literary text they are studying, e.g., subjects from *Romeo and Juliet* could include Passionate Love, Passionate Hate, Rash Swiftness, Star-cross'd Lovers, Parent-Child Relations. They have twenty minutes to complete the project.

2. Give no further instructions, but walk around the room, observing the progress of the various groups. It may be useful to take notes, or tape the discussion in one of the groups. After twenty minutes, each group explains their design and its relation to the subject.
3. As a follow-up, hand out the following questions to be answered by individuals.

   a. How did the group arrive at a decision about what to do?

   b. How did each member contribute ideas?

   c. If some members were quiet, what did group members say or do to encourage participation?

   d. Was there a leader? Was he or she self- or group-appointed?

   e. How was the project organized?

   f. How did the group go about "getting the job done"?

   g. To what extent was frustration shown? How was it expressed?

   h. How did creative abilities of individuals affect the group?

   i. What does the project say about the group's interaction and cooperation?

DAY TWO

1. Students meet with their groups to share answers to the questions. Hand out the following lists for groups to complete using consensus procedures.

   a. List five roles group members might assume. Describe behaviors common to each role.

   b. List five characteristics of leadership that group members might assume.

   c. List five handicaps to the group discussion process.
2. After fifteen minutes, meet in a whole class seminar to combine the groups' lists into a class list of guidelines for member and leader guidelines for behavior. Laminate these class-generated lists and place them on the bulletin board as reminders for desirable cooperative behavior.

WHY THIS WORKS: From this exercise, it is possible to set up classroom criteria for groups to follow. Because the rules are determined by the students themselves, they are more likely to value them. Taking the time to plan guidelines helps to establish patterns of behavior that will minimize future problems.

## DESIGN-A-GAME

OBJECTIVE: Students work cooperatively to apply information they have learned to an activity that is designed as a game.

PROCESS:

1. Divide the class into groups of five. Their job is to create a game for the class to play relating to whatever is currently being studied in the class, or as a review prior to a test.
2. The topics can be punctuation, poetry, prose, vocabulary, or issues relating to characters, plot, or themes. The games can be puzzles, quizzes, scavenger hunts, mystery names or terms, television-type games, or simulations.
3. Criteria for games are established by the nature of the lesson. Evaluation can be based on:

*Product:*

a. Completing project within the set time limit

b. Utilizing all components of the problem

c. Clarity of the game's instructions, including the key or solution if applicable

d. Originality or effectiveness in applying the information

e. Workability

*Process:*

a. All members are actively involved in the planning and the participation.

b. Members display role functions for task and maintenance.

WHY THIS WORKS: Students exercise creativity and learn to value members' contributions as they practice working together. As a review this activity has many benefits for group members and class participants. Students from eighth grade to college level respond well to this activity.

## NOMINAL GROUP TECHNIQUE (NGT)

OBJECTIVE: Students share ideas in a structured interaction that diminishes conflict and provides equal opportunity. The process involves writing thoughts first and then discussing them in a set order. For example, case studies such as "The High School Alcohol Case" can be discussed in this manner. Another possibility would be to use an open question based on literature or current events, such as:

What is the real importance of Caliban in Shakespeare's drama *The Tempest?*

What is the best way to stop the AIDS epidemic among young people today?

PROCESS:

1. Members write ideas out without talking.
2. Each person shares his or her idea in a round-robin fashion. No one questions or challenges the speaker.
3. All ideas are listed on the agenda.
4. Each idea is discussed in turn. Every item receives equal attention.
5. Members silently vote on items to establish priorities.

WHY THIS WORKS: The advantages of this technique are that participation increases and domination by a few vocal personalities is prevented. This format can be varied. Most of the activities in this book, in fact, incorporate aspects of the NGT process. Students write first and share ideas equally. It guarantees more participation and equal access to the conversation.

## SEMINAR

OBJECTIVE: Students in this type of activity discuss ideas first in a small group and then share their findings with a whole class seminar.

PROCESS:

1. Divide the class into groups of three to five people. Give each group one or several open-ended questions to discuss. For literature, the questions can be broad enough to encompass varied texts.

   a. How does the author's life influence his or her subject, theme, or style?

   b. How does setting contribute to the theme, tone, or mood?

   c. Select three images from a poem. How do they reflect the theme and add to the overall effect?

2. After the small groups discuss the questions, they return to the large group to present their findings orally and by means of lists or other tangible products. The activity works best if the class sits in a large circle and the groups sit together. This allows the members of the group to contribute information freely, and lets the rest of the class question, challenge, or submit ideas. Leadership is flexible within groups and each person is equal.

WHY THIS WORKS: Students have an opportunity to speak in the small groups in a way that permits more dialogue. The openness of the format encourages more discussion by individuals.

## THE PANEL

OBJECTIVE: Student members of a panel have a responsibility to contribute ideas and to engage in a discussion in front of an audience.

PROCESS:

1. A panel consists of a leader and four to eight people who discuss a topic informally. Each person presents a different point of view. There are no set speeches, although the members should have prepared in advance. The panel members may speak without being called upon by the

leader; however, the leader should keep the discussion moving, encouraging individuals to contribute and drawing
more reluctant participants into the conversation.

2. Panel members face the audience and remain seated while
talking. Each member makes a short statement about his or
her point of view. Then the discussion ensues: questioning,
expanding, and refuting. At the point where the major
background information has been presented, the leader can
open the discussion to include the whole class.

3. Subjects for discussion can include political issues, school
problems, or open-ended questions from literature or history. The best subjects contain controversy: the development of nuclear power, disarmament, political elections,
the value or interpretation of a particular work of literature.

WHY THIS WORKS: This kind of an activity presents a challenge because students must express their ideas before an audience. Even more difficult is to question and probe for more
information. Students should have a chance to practice their
presentations within their small groups. Although they are
required to have prepared their information beforehand, they
do not need perfect public speaking skills. Thus, while students are prompted to learn the material, they can share the
spotlight with their peers, reducing fear of speaking in public.

## THE SYMPOSIUM

OBJECTIVE: Students present information about a topic to the
class as part of a group. They must plan short talks and be
prepared to answer or ask questions about the topic under
consideration.

PROCESS:

1. Divide the class into groups based on topics of study.
2. Each student prepares a brief formal talk on the subject. All
of the talks within the group should relate to the broader
subject, but develop one facet in more depth.

3. The leader should be selected by the group. His or her job is to coordinate the material and the sequencing of the program.

4. The day of the presentation, the leader explains the topic and the purpose, introduces each speaker, and finally directs the audience questioning session that follows. Speakers may also question each other or add information.

WHY THIS WORKS: This technique is more interesting to the audience than traditional solo oral reports because it involves a majority of the class. The subject matter can range from the explanation of a poem to the background of World War I.

## GROUP CHARACTER STUDY

OBJECTIVE: Students analyze a work of literature through the point of view of a character. Through small groups and as individuals, they explore a character and demonstrate that knowledge through a presentation to the class. (As an example of this method, we will look at the process as it is applied to *Pygmalion* by George Bernard Shaw.)

PROCESS:

1. Students select one of the following characters to study in depth: Higgins, Pickering, Eliza, Mrs. Higgins, Doolittle, Clara.

2. Students join character groups to share information and to practice reading the lines.

*(Student Worksheet with Instructions)*

## *PYGMALION*

Higgins    Pickering    Eliza    Mrs. Higgins    Doolittle    Clara

1. You have been cast in the part of one of the characters. The director has told you to study the character. This means that you are to become totally familiar with not only the character's lines and actions but also with the character's feelings. To do that you are assigned to study all the pertinent lines and

*115*

scenes. Notice how others treat him or her. How does the character react to situations? Is the character quick to action or slow?
Does the character reveal emotions through dialogue or behavior,
or both? How?

2. Take turns reading your character's lines aloud. What kinds of
feelings will he or she have as the action progresses? What kind of
feelings will he or she have about the other characters in the play?
Is he or she sympathetic? Impatient? Understanding? What moti-
vates or inhibits your character?

3. After your study is completed, discuss the following quotes from
your character's point of view. How did you feel at this time in the
play? Why do you feel this way? What do you think others are
feeling? Do you notice their reactions?

> HIGGINS: "The girl doesn't belong to anybody—is no use to
> anybody but me."
>
> "Women upset everything. When you let them get into
> your life, you find the woman is driving at one thing and
> you're driving at another."
>
> PICKERING: "Why don't you marry that missus of yours? I
> rather draw the line at encouraging that sort of immorality."
>
> "If I'm to be in this business I shall feel responsible for
> that girl."
>
> ELIZA: "You're a great bully, you are. I won't stay here if I
> don't like. I won't let nobody wallop me. I never asked to go
> to Bucknam Palace, I didn't. I was never in trouble with the
> police, not me. I'm a good girl—"
>
> "Walk! Not bloody likely. I am going in a taxi."
>
> MRS. HIGGINS: "You certainly are a pretty pair of babies, play-
> ing with your doll."
>
> "She's a triumph of your art and of her dressmaker's; but if
> you suppose for a moment that she doesn't give herself away
> in every sentence she utters, you must be perfectly cracked
> about her."
>
> DOOLITTLE: "Take my advice, Governor: marry Eliza while
> she's young and don't know no better. If you don't you'll be
> sorry for it after. If you do, she'll be sorry for it after; but
> better her than you, because you're a man and she's only a
> woman and don't know how to be happy anyway."

"They played you off very cunning, Eliza, them two sportsmen. If it had been only one of them, you could have nailed him. But you see, there was two; and one of them chaperoned the other, as you might say."

CLARA: "[The new small talk is] all a matter of habit. There's no right or wrong to it. Nobody means anything by it. And it's so quaint, and gives such a smart emphasis to things that are not in themselves very witty. I find the new small talk delightful and quite innocent."

4. Your group will present your character to the class. Each member of your group will share the responsibility of explaining this character to the class. To do this, you will assume the voice of that character and tell about yourself in the first person. We should be able to see the character as a more fully developed person after your presentation. If you wish to use props or costumes to help you "get into" the character, you may.

WHY THIS WORKS: Insights develop as group members share their interpretation of the character. Reading the character's lines aloud helps them to understand the underlying emotions and motivation. A variation of this process is for characters to quiz each other in role or to lead discussions in the persona of their character.

## SELF-ASSESSMENT STRATEGIES

OBJECTIVE: Students learn to assess their role in groups through short or longer, more involved self-reports about their observations and their own behaviors.

PROCESS:

1. Students fill out forms as checklists of behaviors and write informal journals during their group process experiences.
2. Students can share these observations in informal small group talks, whole class discussions, and as part of their own written analysis of the process.

WHY THIS WORKS: These reports increase students' sense of responsibility as part of the group process. The tasks are explicit and the expectations are clear.

---

*Self-Report of Participation*

---

### GROUP PROBLEM-SOLVING EXERCISE

NAME: _____ GROUP NAME: _____

TOPIC: _____

RESEARCH QUESTION: _____

_____

ASSIGNED TASK: As a group, formulate a research question for your topic. Assign individuals specific problem analysis research tasks. During the small group discussions, select and practice specific task and maintenance roles. After discussions, analyze your own behaviors and their effect upon the group's task.

During the discussions, I fulfilled my task functions in the following ways:

Task Function 1. _____

_____

Task Function 2. _____

_____

Task Function 3. _____

_____

During the discussions, I fulfilled my maintenance function(s) in the following ways:

Maintenance 1. _____

_____

Maintenance 2. _____

_____

ANALYSIS: For my part of the research assignment, I contributed the following:

Which task functions helped this group the most? Why?

Which maintenance functions helped this group the most? Why?

*Self-Analysis of Group Process*

NAME: _____

Part 1. Answer the questions in complete sentences as fully as you can. You may use another sheet for your answers.

1. What functional role(s) do you usually play in a group? In this group, what role(s) did you play? Why?
2. Were any roles unfilled (for a time or permanently) in your group? How did this absence affect the group's functioning?
3. How was the important role of information-giver assigned, monitored, and encouraged?
4. Observe your group discussing for ten minutes. Describe the setting for your group and the seating arrangement. Draw a diagram of how the lines of communication extended between the participants.
5. Describe role tasks of your group (leadership tasks, phone calling, keeping records, assigning tasks). List three and explain.
6. Explain how your group built cohesiveness.
7. Explain how your group encouraged participation.
8. How did your group establish leadership? Was the leadership task-oriented or relationship-oriented? What style works better for you?
9. What were some problems your group encountered and how did you overcome them (conflict, time management, record keeping)?
10. What was your research assignment? How/where did you look? What difficulties did you encounter? What resources did you find?

Part 2. Answer the three questions in the form of a journal writing. This writing must be typed.

1. What were the strengths and the weaknesses of your group, as a *group?*
2. What were your own strengths and weaknesses in this group project?
3. What did you learn about yourself and about group communication as a result of this project?

# • Six

## Communication and Reader Response

> The fact that completely different readers can be differently affected by the "reality" of a particular text is ample evidence of the degree to which literary texts transform reading into a creative process that is far above mere perception of what is written.                    —Iser

$C$lassroom talk has particular value for improving reading comprehension. Reading a text aloud, discussing its meanings, and interpreting characters' roles are all activities that fit under the broad category of reader response. Readers shape meaning as they move from concrete personal experiences to abstractions of those experiences. This kind of thinking is essential for perceptive, competent readers. And these understandings become more accessible to all students through classroom talk and through creative dramatic activities. As Ginny, a twelfth grade student, observes in her journal:

> It was interesting to see different interpretations of the same character by different groups. Many interpretations focused on a single aspect of the character, different from all the rest, but pertaining to the same basic trait. For example, Heathcliff was always the "bad guy." Each group which portrayed the character always portrayed him as such. Yet different groups focused on different aspects of his evil. Colleen showed Heathcliff's ability to make Hindley jealous; Lisa showed how Heathcliff was an unwelcome intruder into the Linton home.

# A Definition of Reader Response

Reader response is a classroom practice. It is also a valid form of literary criticism. Reader response allows readers to develop meaning as they interact with a text (Chase and Hynd 1987; Holbrook 1987). The text is not just an object containing a "correct" meaning, and the reader is not just someone working to decipher the author's intent. Instead, readers *work* with the text to create a meaning. The text is an experience. "The reader's response is not *to* the meaning; it *is* the meaning" (Fish 1980, 3). Changing the focus of meaning to the individual involves looking at the process of reading and the acts that the reader performs as central to understanding. The relationships between interpretation and text create the shape of reading. Because this interaction shapes reading, it also shapes the text rather than the text shaping the interaction, as we often assume (Fish 1980).

Reading, a highly complex process, involves more than the passive recognition of words. It also encompasses understanding the concepts behind those words. To fully comprehend, readers have to fit new information from a text into their own world view. The child from a rural environment, for example, may lack background experience to understand *subway system*. A foreign student may have no comparable experience for *cheerleader*. Simply decoding words and locating contextual references are insufficient when readers deal with unfamiliar ideas.

A community of learners, using discovery methods, can enhance one another's concept building. They share their perceptions and interpretive strategies. Someone in the rural school may have visited a city and experienced a subway ride. Small discussion groups inform the foreign student about the mystique of cheerleaders. Readers are trained to look first within themselves at their own experience and to value that knowledge. Interpersonal sharing, coupled with intrapersonal reflection, unlocks hidden clues from a text. Students share memories, other readings, historical references, and questions as part of their interaction with a text. As they discuss and question, they build a bridge of understanding between the text and their own lives in a manner not possible when all the questions originate from the teacher.

## *Connecting Reader and Text*

The goal of reader response in the classroom is to facilitate students' perceptions and responses to a text rather than to dictate a specific view. Louise Rosenblatt (1978, 12) describes the interaction between reader and text as a transaction that creates a "poem," her term for any literary work of art.

> The poem, then, must be thought of as an event in time. It is not an object or an ideal entity. It happens during a coming-together, a compenetration of a reader and a text. The reader brings to the text his past experience and present personality. Under the magnetism of the ordered symbols of the text, he marshals his resources and crystallizes out from the stuff of memory, thought, and feeling a new order, a new experience, which he sees as the poem.

The reader's penetration into the author's world creates a peculiar demand. The two worlds must connect. The reader has to imagine the unfamiliar world of the author's design. Wolfgang Iser (1974, 279) describes that imaginative process as constructing "a virtual dimension of the text." This virtual dimension is not the objective text itself, nor is it the reader's fantasy. It is a product of the combined thoughts.

Additionally, individual meanings have intrinsic worth for the students. Linking events in the text to their own lives helps build meaning and aids memory retention. Reader response also allows readers to define their own lives. Hamlet's struggles become part of the explanation for their own indecisions. Nora in *A Doll's House* strives to learn her own identity, but she forces all of us to look inside ourselves as well. From the diversity of perspectives a vast number of interpretative choices emerges.

*123*

## The Reading Process

The successful reading process thus involves becoming more deeply involved with the text. Ciardi calls this act "participation." "By participating, the reader not only makes the performance whole, but makes it, in one essential sense, uniquely his" (Ciardi and Williams 1975, 12). The reading process is not a passive reception of ideas; instead, it is the very active experience of making meaning.

The word *experience* connotes living through an event with all of its attendant difficulties. More than just appreciation, experiencing literature involves struggling with meaning, puzzling out conflicts, and feeling with and for characters. The reader, no less than a participant in an actual event, must ask questions and gather additional information. Why does the author use this setting? Why does the character say those words? What does this metaphor signify? "Experiencing fully is the way to understand most fully" (O'Keefe 1988a, 38).

As teachers we must recognize that there are many dimensions of understanding for a work of art. The literary critic reads in one dimension; the history scholar reads in another; the eighth grader in still another. The goal for readers at any level is to improve their perceptions. Communities of readers in a classroom who share their experiences move toward more complete knowledge. The goal of reader response is to begin that journey. Making connections to the text and each other's experiences forges "literacy links" that strengthen comprehension for the whole community.

## Talk Increases Comprehension

Informally chatting about stories improves students' capacity to form conceptions about a text, a necessary step in the all-important job of comprehension. National studies have shown that students are quick to give initial ideas about what they have read, but few are able to explain these ideas through reference either to the text or to their own feelings or opinions.

Text → Exemplification → Generalization → Abstract Thought

Figure 2: *Discussing Examples*

When asked for a discussion of the theme or main idea, the most frequent response that students give is a summary or synopsis of the text. One conclusion is that students are adept at formulating quick, brief interpretations. What they lack is experience in formulating longer, more involved responses to literature (*Education Research Report* 1992).

## Ability to Abstract

Students lose out in several ways when talk is curtailed. If they can discuss examples, describe analogies, and retell similar experiences as they read literature, they increase their ability to create inferences and find themes or main ideas. Their reading comprehension increases (Wittrock 1984). According to Applebee (1978), granting time for discussing examples, or exemplification, produces the most advanced ability, building of meaning beyond the words in the text (see Figure 2).

Projecting what happens after the story ends or imagining what events might have preceded the story's beginning allows students to construct an ongoing depiction of the story, providing a framework for inference. In other words, through talking about literature and relating it to their own lives, students increase their capacity for abstraction. The abilities to generalize and abstract are functions of higher-order thinking and critical thought. Critical thinking in its most holistic sense is thinking that involves more abstract operations.

Projecting ideas from a text into their own experiences demands sophistication. Readers are required to explore how the work interacts with their view of the world. They may find that they agree or disagree with the author's point of view. The text may provide some personal insight or trigger a memory. Students often want to talk about the problem of alcoholism when they read *Wuthering Heights*. When students discuss Heathcliff's threatening Nelly with a knife, the incident can be generalized to issues of power, greed, and domestic violence. Most significant, however, is that student talk enhances the quality of abstraction. The implications for this finding are vast, faced as we are with low test scores and achievement deficiencies. Heterogeneous classrooms provide a rich climate for raising the shared experience level for all students.

The experienced reader follows cues and clues in the text to discern meaning. The less experienced reader may miss those signs and become confused. Sharing ideas in discussion helps both types of students. The more able benefit from articulation of their thoughts, and the less able perceive possible approaches to understanding. Both also gain from the sharing of different perspectives.

## Shared Experiences

It is interesting to observe what students are capable of doing when faced with the problem of discerning the meaning of a text without a teacher's direct guidance. The following is a transcript of a group of twelfth grade students discussing *Wuthering Heights*. They were alone in a room with just a tape recorder. The transcript illustrates how they struggle to relate Heathcliff's character to their existing knowledge.

JAN: Is he [Heathcliff] influenced more by heredity or environment?

GINNY: We don't know what his heredity was!

JAN: Let's assume it to be the Earnshaw family, okay?

GINNY: No, no, no. For environment, yes, but heredity is anybody's guess. Environment, it's obvious, yes. If you grew up with everyone beating you . . .

LORI: Just think about his heredity as when he first came to the family. He wasn't the mean kind of kid. He was—

GINNY: Yeah, he was silent.

JESSIE: Then he became all revengeful.

LORI: Hindley had such an influence over him that he almost became like Hindley was, if not worse.

GINNY: Then again, heredity must have had something to do, because after Hindley's influence is gone, he was still maturing—and he just—I mean that vengefulness in him couldn't have come from Hindley. That's what makes me think—this is really weird—but, don't laugh—the Italians—that's where the word *vendetta* comes from—the Sicilians because the Mediterranean people are so. . .

JAN: Vindictive?

GINNY: No, their emotions are so intense. I don't know why. It's the Latin people, their emotions are most intense, and this is so weird. Let's just assume now, the theory, if Heathcliff was from a gypsy, that was his heritage, then we would have this same characteristic.

LORI: Which would cause him to overreact as he tended to do.

GINNY: And that coupled with his environment . . .

JAN: Yeah!

The students' talk helps to broaden their experiences. Jan is apparently unsure of the significance of heredity, or perhaps the meaning of the term. Together they work at defining a problem and reflecting on the causes for Heathcliff's personality. Ginny observes that Heathcliff was a gypsy. Thus, his nature was wild, and that, coupled with Hindley's abuse, accounts for his vengeance. We see the emergence of inference and abstraction. Ginny, under challenge by the other students, infers a connection between Heathcliff and the word *vendetta*, and with her own prior knowledge, she forms a hypothesis. Her conclusion is not contrary to critics who note the natural wildness of Heathcliff which, depending on the writer, signifies fantasy, natural goodness corrupted, or Earnshaw's infidelity.

## Knowledge of Story Structure

Aside from lack of background experience and ability to expand ideas, another barrier to reading comprehension exists, a sense of narrative. Story-telling and narrative are

*127*

natural ways that adults communicate and make sense of their lives. We consistently talk our way through the various disastrous and joyous events of our lives, from snow storms to new babies. Children, too, use this skill. As early as two and a half, young children can form monologues and commence telling stories. Not only that, they also recognize that stories are different from ordinary language. As three-year-old Maggie says, "I'm just tending," as she begins to weave another fanciful tale.

Applebee (1978) has identified six basic types of structures in the stories told by children from two to five: heaps, sequences, primitive narratives, unfocused chains, focused chains, and narratives. Each type, according to Applebee, is a more advanced level of structure than the one before. (This view is questioned by Orlando Taylor [1990], who claims that story structure is culture-bound, and thus perhaps presents a reason for comprehension problems in some groups of children.) These findings support the need for children to experience oral narratives. If Western literature is sequential, children have to become accustomed to those patterns and traditions.

Familiarity with story-telling is a prerequisite for understanding a text, and sharing stories aloud should not end with elementary school. Simple narratives may present few difficulties, but complex structures with flashbacks, interior monologues, or embedded information invariably create confusions, even in secondary classrooms. The more practice students have in telling and hearing stories, the easier their task will be when reading stories and dramas with unaccustomed patterns. Explicit instruction in story "grammar" can help low-performing and learning disabled students (Gersten and Dimino 1989).

Students' comprehension increases when they are taught to ask themselves questions while reading. They learn to question characters' personalities and motives, obstacles, expected outcomes, and themes. Children's performances can significantly improve when teachers model aloud the way to ask questions and to find answers, and then allow students to practice the method. Average children, as well as low achievers, can use story grammars to look for plot elements, symbolic images, and character development as part of study group work. Thus talking *about* narratives, as well as telling them, reinforces understanding about what a story means and does.

The less experienced reader can benefit from more signposts about structure. However, modeling narrative-telling and directed instruction in story grammar are not just techniques for less skilled readers. Most children have trouble understanding ambiguous references, the implied knowledge of allusions, or vaguely stated relationships between events or people. Therefore, all students need strategies to help recognize a story's subtle message, conflicts, theme, and character motivations. Allowing time for students to discuss their findings with their peers increases their awareness of strategies they can use alone.

## Reader Response Strategies

Practicing the skills of reader response requires time and planning. Teachers have to decide what activities will build meaning, design the logistics, and monitor the outcomes. However, they reap the advantages of increased student participation and a greater level of achievement for all ability levels. Sharing ideas, advancing theories, developing questions, and creating imaginative situations contribute to making connections between life and literature. In addition, students develop a sense of ownership and confidence about their powers to understand.

### Oral Reading

One way to increase familiarity with narrative is to read literature aloud. Talking *about* literature increases knowledge explicitly. Reading literature aloud increases knowledge implicitly and is a most effective form of reader response. Sensitive reading of a text conveys its many levels of meaning.

The model for this kind of reading is first of all the teacher. As she savors the sound and the excitement of a piece of literature, she imparts not only understanding of a work, but also her joy.

Students should also read aloud in a variety of ways: round-robin, chorus, dialogue, duo, monologue, and readers' theater. When readers approach a confusing text as storytellers themselves, they relate better to the author's purpose and task. Students become familiar with the conventions of storytelling when they interpret stories aloud or tell narratives themselves.

## Modeling Mental Processes

Another method of reader response involves modeling the mental processes one uses to extract meaning from a difficult text. Different from modeling questions in a story grammar, this system calls for expressing thoughts about meaning line by line. It is an initial interaction with a text. A cognitive modeling activity at the end of this chapter describes the process more fully.

The benefit of such an activity mirrors I. A. Richard's (1929) discovery: the wonderful diversity of impressions. No longer will the meaning of the text be confined to one (probably the teacher's) reading of the literature. Yet through the shared ideas, a common thread emerges, assisting in building a meaningful explanation. Certain principles should guide this kind of exercise. There are no predetermined right or wrong answers. As in life, students are allowed to take risks and to make mistakes. They are also able to make associations. Thus responses may take different forms—such as: "This reminds me of . . . ," "I see a picture of . . . ," or "I really am not sure, but I think . . ."

Through modeling, students begin to see the conventions of storytelling and to experience narrative's diversity. James Britton (1970, 110) has called literature written gossip. We are all natural storytellers, and we need to build on that skill in order to recognize a repertoire of narrative styles. Literature, with its complex intertwining of ideas, requires a vast array of cognitive skills: recall, prediction, projection—to name a few. And all of these skills must operate concurrently. Yet we find if we concentrate too much on these skills, the sense of the passage may be lost, much as the bicyclist may fall when she thinks about her balance. Just as the bicyclist once learned to ride, we must practice the cognitive skills until they become second nature.

## Writing Prompts Discussion

In order to foster whole class participation, it helps if students write responses before discussions. Writing, by itself, is a link to improved comprehension. Research is showing that not only do we learn to read better by reading and learn to write better by writing, we learn to read by writing and to write by reading (Goodman and Goodman 1984). Students who write and talk to make meaning have better access to a literary text. Youngblood (1985) describes his success with students' use of a reading journal. The reading journal is an interactive text. The student jots down thoughts, observations, and questions as she reads. The journal serves as a reflection of the on-going process of making meaning. Students engage more actively in reading when they write informally about their thoughts. "It is important that students write as they read, as ideas and thoughts occur to them. Getting thoughts, ideas, and feelings down is important; otherwise they're lost" (p. 46).

Students using the reading journal, as well as other kinds of speaking and writing activities, become involved with translating the text "out there" into a personally meaningful experience for themselves. They may write informally about questions, confusions, speculations, or creative reactions. Sometimes students may write a monologue in the role of a character, compare the character's life to their own, or compose a poem or story as a response. Monica sorts out some of her confusions with a response to a word from the novel *The Heart of the Matter:*

> When I first began to read and saw the word "nigger" I found it inappropriate considering [the author] is supposed to be

*131*

a contemporary writer. But then I realized that it wasn't because Graham Greene was prejudiced or was trying to make blacks look bad, he was just expressing the way that white men felt during that time, and was just setting the scene and making it more authentic.

Anne, another student, is confused about the living conditions in *1984*, by George Orwell:

It seems like the author is describing the past in some ways. The author combines the technology of the future with the rundown conditions of the past. . . . Society does not seem to be progressing. . . . It seems to be more primitive than today. . . . The language becoming smaller with words cut out limits the thoughts of the people and makes the people themselves more primitive.

Sometimes students select a phrase for response, as has Elise:

"I have not broken your heart—you have broken it, and in breaking it, you have broken mine."
    Heathcliff speaks [these words] to Catherine as she is dying, expressing to her how hurt he is that the time in their life has been wasted on breaking each others' hearts instead of spending quality time loving each other. Now Catherine and Heathcliff have to live with a guilt, and when she dies he will carry it alone.

In-role writing affords a way to get into the character's skin. Here Maureen takes on the persona of Marnie in Doris Lessing's short story "The Witness," and with that exploration she finds that the character's choice was perhaps a miserable one:

I'm engaged to be married to Mr. Jones. I guess I'm happy—I have my whole life ahead of me and when I told my family that I was marrying Tom [Mr. Jones], my father was so happy. He told me I had found a good fish in the sea. I don't want my husband to be fish. I want him to be the man I love. . . .

## Sharing Responses

Journal writing allows individuals to discover their personal reactions to a text, but to broaden the perspective, the journals must be shared with a partner, a small group, or the class. It is often better if students have written several entries to allow a choice of material to share. When they have all written in the role of a character, it is enlightening to see how the characters have been perceived by other classmates. As students meet in small groups, everyone has a greater chance to be heard than in a whole class discussion. A recorder in each group can keep track of the members' reactions. This ordering of ideas aids in the report back to the class. Any number of methods can be used to organize the information as a presentation to the whole class: charts, collages, readings, panel discussions, interviews, or simply the recorder reporting her notes.

Given the responsibilities of writing, discussing, and reporting to the class, students rise to the occasion of helping each other in study groups. Moira, writing a reaction to her group's discussion about *Wuthering Heights*, reveals its members' ability to puzzle out Brontë's sometimes ambiguous text:

> Today in class in our discussion group we cleared up a lot of *Wuthering Heights* that I was originally having trouble understanding. . . . We figured out that there were two Catherines. . . .

Another student, Celia, found help understanding Graham Greene's *The Heart of the Matter:*

> By being in our group I understand the story a little better. . . . I think Wilson is a spy who is checking up on the police in Africa and by getting close to Louise he can find out more information.

Besides engaging in small group and whole class discussion, students can have dialogue response in pairs, or Pen Pals as they call it. Students are paired with a partner. They read each others' journals, write responses to their partners, and discuss ideas once or twice a week. A sample interchange concerning the novel *1984* between two twelfth grade students illustrates how this works.

> ANNE: To start out with, I thought you were just going to summarize too much. You do seem to be getting away from summary toward the end of your writing which is good. . . . You mentioned

that the proles did not like the government. I saw them as being indifferent to it.

EDWARD: I don't think I was summarizing. I was just saying what happened. You brought up some good comments like the proles were indifferent to the government. . . . The proles were indifferent to the world they lived in. . . .

Note Anne's remarks about Edward's summarizing, the most common type of response noted in national assessments, as well as Edward's answer. "Just saying what happened" in Edward's mind is not summarizing. Nevertheless, a peer's remarking on this form of writing, or thinking, is probably more effective than a teacher's comments. If students learn to self-correct and to help others, they are weaned away from simply retelling events. Learning to generalize, abstract, and form conclusions is a movement toward higher cognitive function.

Other examples of pen pal responses attest to their benefit.

JILL: [Concerning the novel *1984*] At times I was a little confused by the Brotherhood but just by reading your response I understand it better now. It is interesting to see what someone else thought of the same book.

DONALD: [Concerning the novel *Heart of the Matter*] Kristen, as I read through the book, I found that your response to my question was correct. Louise left for South Africa because she was unhappy with life. Everybody hated her and she wanted to experience a new environment.

Through oral and written reader responses, the teacher has a clearer window on the students' comprehension problems. Without feedback, the teacher, as a more experienced reader, may not always pinpoint areas of difficulty for her younger readers. She may not realize that students do not know the meaning of the word *remission*, for instance, when they are reading *Eric* by Doris Lund. A journal entry or a discussion may reveal just such a difficulty. Students may not recognize a time period. They may think *To Kill a Mockingbird* takes place before the Civil War. They may surmise that Nelly is a black servant in *Wuthering Heights,* or they may assume that Winston is actually shot at the end of *1984.* Eliciting their responses allows errors to be corrected promptly, if not by their study groups, then by the teacher. These response-sharing sessions promote greater interest and at the same time become self-correcting procedures.

## Using Dramatic Interpretation

So far we have looked at activities focused on informal writing and talking, but a performance type of response may be used during or after reading a text. These responses involve students' generating creative dramatizations of scenes or character reactions. They can be as simple as improvisations of situations, or they can be more developed overviews of a whole work. One of the major effects of dramatic activities is that students have a chance to decenter, an aid to the abstraction of ideas. Decentering is the movement away from egocentric, personal thought, to other-centered vision (Moffett 1968; Elkind 1981), and this movement allows abstraction to occur.

Dramatic response is generally enjoyed by participants and audience. Some postdrama evaluations by students contain comments such as, "You have to think and be like the character," "I have to study the character more as I read," "I looked for places where 'I' appeared," and "I hadn't thought about characters and motivations with such depth before."

Students can chart the journey of a character through a novel by dramatizing certain events, selecting scenes that illustrate conflict or theme, writing original scripts that depict dramatic events, or composing monologues for certain characters. In a ninth grade class, students were paired with partners to generate dialogue from a scene in the novel *To Kill a Mockingbird.* The students were to write a dialogue of approximately a page between two characters. They read these short scripts to the class, providing both a review of plot action and character interpretation. And perhaps more importantly, they were given an opportunity to rephrase events in their own language.

A sample script by P. G. and Allan illustrates this kind of interpretation in the following scene between Cecil and Scout:

SCOUT: You better take that back or I'ma kick yo hiney!

CECIL: Shut up girl you can't do nuttin.

SCOUT: Boy my fists are just boiling with steam and all I wanna do is punch your lights out.

CECIL: Yo daddy defend them negros.

SCOUT: You lying, you lyin Cecil Jacobs.

CECIL: No I ain't. Yo daddy ain't nuttin but a nigger lover.

SCOUT: Boy, you done did it know [sic] Im ready to knock yo butt.

CECIL: Go on little girl you can't do nuttin.

SCOUT: Jem, stop don't hold me back—no don't hold me back Im ready to fight.

CECIL: Let her go Jem she ain't gonna do nuttin.

SCOUT: Cecil Jacobs your a lucky one because I was gonna rearrange yo face.

The script that emerged from the above activity sounds very much like a natural "playing the dozens," a kind of verbal test of strength that one might hear in the school cafeteria. The value of this exercise is, then, a chance for students to "practice" the characters' emotional confrontation on their own terms. One group in a class studying *Wuthering Heights* chose to write monologues, using Nelly, young Catherine, and Emily Brontë. Melanie wrote in her journal about the experience:

The main key to our project was a lot of talking. Shirley and I discussed characteristics of the characters one day over lunch and noticed that each of the women had characteristics of willfulness. We wrote interior monologues, then, to exemplify and to compare that trait. . . . Then we got into discussing isolation as an influencing factor on willfulness.

Speaking and acting forced the students to live the emotions of the characters, bringing the text to life, as Beth described in her journal:

The project helped me because when we were acting out our scene, I could feel the rage in Heathcliff. I could feel the disgust he had for Linton and the desire for revenge on Edgar. These things drove him, and I could feel that force when I was saying his words. When I was playing Linton, I could feel his fear. I could feel his need for Catherine and his need for her as a shield. I think that putting a scene in motion helps us *see* characters and *know* them.

Speaking in role promotes more abstract thinking abilities in children. Abstract thinking skills are dependent both upon maturation and classroom techniques. Some researchers believe, as did Piaget (1966), that until children have reached the age of fourteen or so and achieved "formal operations," they are unable to cope adequately with abstractions. Lacking that stage of development, children may have difficulty making inferences or hypothesizing. Engaging in dramatic role playing demands decentering and making the leap into formal operations. The secondary classroom can become the catalyst to foster *both* the skills and the learning stage as students are stretched beyond their natural limits into the realm Vygotsky (1979) called the zone of proximal development. Drama, by its nature, is ideally suited to accomplish these tasks. The almost-real world of drama means that an individual can live safely under several hats, experiencing others' feelings and viewpoints.

If as a teacher you doubt the claims I am making for writing, speaking, and thinking in role, I suggest that you experiment with these activities yourself. I have found amazing insights pop into my head when I embark on these adventures with my students.

## Reader Response Is a Motivator

All of the kinds of reader response described above have a strong underlying component: to activate the learner in the process of understanding. As Martin (1976) explains, "active learning" refers less to finding information for yourself than what you do with it when you have found it. Most importantly, it should be remembered that reader response evolves from the learners themselves. Discovering what background needs enrichment, providing ample time for exemplification, allowing risk-taking, and facilitating dramatic as well as discussion responses are teacher functions. This kind of environment is never boring for the students or the teacher. The added bonus is that comprehension and critical thinking skills are also improved.

Students as they engage in reader response oral activities draw on their personal opinions and reactions. This creativity sparks a willingness to invest more energy in the effort of reading than do more traditional methods. Placing the responsibility for learning on the individual raises curiosity and enthusiasm for the task. Peer pressure encourages students to measure up to group expectations, not just teacher-set goals. As they listen to other students talk about a text in the language and terms of their own lives, the personal risks of engaging with literature are reduced. Talking and listening form an essential link between the text out there and the learner within. The method is reader response; the strategies are as broad as the teacher's and students' imagination allows.

*Teacher-Researcher Questions*
1. How might modeling self-questioning aloud while reading a text affect students' performance?
2. What kinds of prompts for students' expressive speech or journals contribute to their understanding of text?
3. How can reading journals contribute to building a community of readers?
4. How might dramatic reader response aid student perceptions of characters?

# • *ACTIVITIES* •

## READER RESPONSE PROMPTS

OBJECTIVE: Students are given an incentive to frame an original response to the literature. From these writings they can develop meaning. In turn, the writings are the source for talking to learn.

PROCESS:

1. *You are a character.* Write a diary entry about your feelings during an event in the novel. Describe the situation, the people involved, and explore how you were affected.
2. *Pen Pals.* Write a letter to another student in the class asking a question or making an observation about a character or situation in a novel. Answer the letter you receive. Meet with your pen pal to discuss your responses.
3. *Select-a-phrase.* Choose a phrase from the first page of a novel, play, or short story. Write the phrase and underline key words. Explain why this phrase is significant to the plot, tone, or characterization of the story.
4. *Question-Response.* Write a puzzling question about a fact, theme, or plot. Answer your question in a one-page response. The correct answer is not the purpose of this response; exploring possibilities is the goal.
5. *Matching Experiences.* Describe an incident in your own life that matches one in the story.
6. *Ending Change.* What if the ending were changed? How would you rewrite it?
7. *Diagram-an-Idea.* Draw a diagram or a sketch of a scene in the story. Explain why you selected the scene and the meaning of the sketch. (For instance, Room 101 in *1984*)
8. *Fan Letter.* Write a letter to a character or the author, explaining what about her, him, or the story you like or do not like. Ask questions about their decisions or actions. Compare their lives to your own.

9. *Novel Games.* Make up a game for the novel. What are the rules? Who would play? Design the board or playing field.

10. *Character Letter.* You are a character in the novel. Write the author about his or her treatment of you. Or write the reader to explain why you might have been misunderstood.

11. *Free Verse.* Select a word or phrase from a novel or poem and write a free verse poem reflecting the mood of the literature.

12. *Meet the Characters.* Describe the characters as they were five years before the beginning of the story.

13. *Minor Character View.* Choose a minor character. How does this character interact with the main character? How does this interaction affect the main character or the plot?

14. *Theme.* What is the author saying? What values are important in this story? Do these values apply to your life?

15. *Conflict.* Select a scene and show how this develops the conflict of the story. Compare the conflict to a current event today.

WHY THIS WORKS: These prompts stimulate the imagination and generate original ways to look at a text. They also provide fruitful material for discussions in small groups and seminars.

## ROLE WRITING-SPEAKING

OBJECTIVE: Students write in first person as a character in a poem, play, or fiction writing in order to recast the material in a new mode for better understanding.

PROCESS: (The following instructions suggest an approach to "Who's Who," by W. H. Auden.)

1. Students silently read the poem. Then a volunteer or the teacher reads the poem aloud.

2. The class is divided in half. One half is the "great man." Their instructions are to write the following, using the first person:

   a. You have just climbed Mt. Everest or have just returned from your Antarctic expedition. Write a letter to the someone you "sigh for" telling how you feel or what you have done or thought.

   b. The other half of the class is the "someone." Their instructions are to write the following, using the first person:

   c. It is a typical day at your home. Write a letter to the great man, telling him what you've been doing, what you are thinking and feeling.

3. After writing for about ten minutes, the students form a large circle. The "great men" sit on one side, and the "someones" on the other. Alternate readings of letters. Next ask the "great men" if they have any questions for the "someones" and vice versa.

4. Read the poem aloud again. Ask students to write a brief response to the poem again as if they had received a letter from the other person. What is their feeling now?

5. The discussion can continue with students' reading their responses, formulating questions or making simple statements about their feelings about the poem. It is important to accept the free responses so that students will be able to generate opinions without a feeling that they will be judged on the rightness or the wrongness of answers.

WHY THIS WORKS: When students decenter by assuming another personality, they enter into that character's world. This activity allows the readers to experience the poem. Variations: For Shelley's "Ozymandias," students can write in the role of Ozymandias, the traveler, or the speaker. The speaker can write a letter home, the traveler can write a diary entry, and Ozymandias can compose an interior monologue. For Keats' "Ode on a Grecian Urn," students can assume the character of the youth, the maiden, the priest, and the urn itself. What are their thoughts as contrasted to the speaker?

## READING INCENTIVE: NOVEL READING RECORDS

OBJECTIVE: Encouraging students to increase the quantity of reading through records makes the activity tangible.

PROCESS:

1. Once a week students have a twenty-minute free reading time. At the end of this reading time, students fill in a reading record, recording the date, book title, and pages completed for the week.
2. As a way to get started on a class novel, students read for twenty minutes for a succession of days, keeping a daily record.
3. In addition, students write a predetermined number of reader responses that allow them to comment about intriguing, puzzling, or pleasing features of the text.
4. Credit can be assigned for completing the novel(s). Students who do not complete a novel can receive credit based on the percentage of the novel read.
5. Every other week students meet informally with partners or groups to discuss their readings.

WHY THIS WORKS: Since class time is not sufficient to complete a novel, students are encouraged indirectly to read outside of class. Students have a visible record of their efforts, and discussions with classmates invariably involve their reading progress. Slow starters are thus stimulated to try harder. If the records involve a common literary text, reading and discussing responses from later parts of the novel is a motivator to read the literature.

## HOW A POEM ACTS

OBJECTIVE: Through dramatic performance students will understand the feelings and the meaning of a poem.

PROCESS:

1. Select poems that have some movement, sounds, or emotions. Good poems for this activity are "At Grass," by Philip Larkin; "The Thought-Fox," by Ted Hughes; "The Animals' Arrival," by Elizabeth Jennings; and "Refugee Blues," by W. H. Auden.
2. Read the poems aloud with the class first. Practice informally with different readers and sound effects. Encourage students to move their bodies to get a kinesthetic feel for the words.
3. Divide the class into groups of four or five people. Give each group a different poem with enough copies so that every member has one.
4. Groups plan a dramatic presentation of their poem. There are no rules about how the presentation will be performed except that each member must have an active role.
5. Groups are allowed about ten minutes to prepare. In that time, they listen for sounds as well as meaning. They think about motions and sound effects and where they should sit, stand, or lie as they present the poem. Then they should read the poem aloud and practice their performance several times.
6. Groups return to the whole class and present their poems in turn.
7. Allow time for discussion to follow the presentations so that students can question meanings and interpretations.
8. Variations of this plan can include more preparation time for sound and light performances. Students can read poetry accompanied by music and/or a backdrop of slides or opaque projections. Original poetry or collections of poems by the same author can be produced.

WHY THIS WORKS: Presenting poetry demands an understanding of the connotation of words. Students recognize the emotional quality of words and rhythms when they have to think about their presentations. As an audience they can hear the meanings and see the movement, building a deeper appreciation for the art (O'Keefe 1988a).

## BECOME-A-CHARACTER

OBJECTIVE: Students experience a literary or historical event through role-playing a character, thus developing a capacity to decenter and to make inferences.

PROCESS:

1. Divide the class into groups of four or five people. Assign each group one character from the literary text.
2. As that character, students write in role a ten-minute free response to a prompt. Tell them to write using "I," not "he" or "she." At this point they don't discuss the character with other group members, so it is better if they have not actually moved their chairs into a group formation.

   Suggested prompt examples are:

   *Julius Caesar*
   You are Caesar. Write a monologue addressed to Antony about your past successes, future plans, and concerns.

   *Pygmalion*
   You are Eliza. Write a diary about your experiences with Professor Henry Higgins and why you chose to study with him.

   *Wuthering Heights*
   You are Heathcliff. Write a monologue addressed to Nellie about why you left Wuthering Heights and where you went for your three-year disappearance.
3. Meet in groups to discuss your character and your responses. Each person reads his or her response to the group. Following these readings, discuss the similarities and differences among the members' versions.
4. Next, each group generates one or two questions to ask the other characters. The questions also must be in first person in the role of their character.

5. Return to the large circle. If the text were *Julius Caesar*, all the Caesars would be in one section, the Brutuses in another, and so forth for the other characters. Beginning with Caesar, each student in that group would read or tell his thoughts as Caesar. Then the other characters would ask Caesar questions from their point of view. Brutus might ask Caesar if he really would accept a crown at some future time. Any Caesar could answer; all should be encouraged to reply. Next the focus would move to Brutus. The same method of reading and questioning is repeated until all characters have responded. This kind of activity builds a mood and momentum that is hard to recapture a second day. For that reason, it is best to keep a lively pace.

6. Numerous variations of this activity are possible, moving to improvisation scenes between characters, switching Caesars and Brutuses, for example, to explore different emotions and meanings.

WHY THIS WORKS: Students enjoy this activity. Beneath the fun are deeper levels of meaning. Character motivations and personalities emerge, fleshing out figures from the classics, especially for the less experienced reader (O'Keefe 1988a).

## CREATION STORIES

OBJECTIVE: Students experience the value of storytelling by studying creation stories and myths. Creation stories reflect a people's ways of explaining themselves in relation to the world.

PROCESS:

1. Students can research and find their own creation stories for comparison.
2. Research should include more than the stories themselves. An effort should be made to find the cultural values of the people and their history to put the tale into the context of their socio-history. These projects can take the form of storytelling, skits, or puppet shows.

<u>WHY THIS WORKS</u>: Students become engaged in a discovery project to learn about stories and the people that generated them.

## NATIVE AMERICAN STORIES

<u>OBJECTIVE</u>: Students read Native American stories from a different perspective than Western chronological narrative and discover possible meanings based on their personal responses.

<u>PROCESS</u>:

1. Native American tribes often have stories that include the trickster Coyote. Coyote may be in conflict with Earthman, Buzzard, or Frog Woman. We should not read these Native American stories the way we read our own literature. They are not in chronological time. The stories are intended as a way to make sense of our lives as we live them. The stories change in meaning as we change, and the meanings are different for each individual.
2. Students can read and then discuss the following tale to discover what meaning it holds for them.

### Wintu Coyote Story
#### Told by the Wintu Indians of Northern California

Buzzard was busy building a tower. This tower was going to be so high it would reach to heaven. While Buzzard worked hard at his task, Coyote approached Hoos, for that was the Buzzard's name. He asked, "Hoos, what are you doing?" Hoos answered Sedit, the coyote, "I am building a tower to heaven so folks on earth can see the people up there. They can get strength from them. Old people will get new life and come back down to earth."

Sedit thought that was a silly thing to do. "People have to die. If people keep coming back from heaven, the earth will get too crowded." With that wise pronouncement he pushed over the tower. Then he saw Hoos fly away, high up in the sky.

Sedit said, "Wait! Wait! I want to follow you. I'll make myself some wings!"

So he made wings out of sunflower leaves and put them on his arms. Then the coyote jumped up and tried to fly, but he could not. He fell back, stunned.

Buzzard came back and saw him and said, "I am going to that mountain east of this place to live. You? I don't know where you will live."

So the mountain, Hoosbooli, is the home of the buzzards, while coyotes live everywhere and have no special home. (Adapted from Masson 1990)

WHY THIS WORKS: The meaning is based on one's own life. Discussing this story unveils our values and those of the Wintus.

## MYTH LIBRARY

OBJECTIVE: Building a classroom library of myths and finding their meanings is another way to develop an awareness of diverse world views.

PROCESS: Students contribute stories, poems, and legends from their own and other cultures. These can become a resource for writing or reference.

WHY THIS WORKS: Students learn to value the multicultural heritage we enjoy with our diversity. These stories build an understanding of narrative and also build their experience base of others' world views.

## COGNITIVE MODELING

OBJECTIVE: Individuals share aloud the way they process meaning from symbolic language or as problem solving. Cognitive modeling is a helpful strategy because it gives students a view of how others process information.

PROCESS:

1. The method is to talk aloud about a problem, an unfamiliar work of literature, a vocabulary word in context, or any

other event that needs "figuring out." This outer speech can then become the students' inner speech when faced with solving problems alone.

2. The teacher begins the process, usually, taking the risk in talking about the unfamiliar and relating it to the known in a spontaneous way. Students are encouraged to continue the process in a systematic way, taking turns talking aloud. Poetry can be cognitively modeled line by line, with each student taking a line and giving his or her impression of the meaning. Or students can form dyads and alternate lines, preferably after the teacher has paired with a student to model the technique. Small groups can be formed to share the meanings derived by combining two dyads, and then the whole class can combine their findings.

3. An example of cognitive modeling for the title and first lines of Linda Pastan's (1988) poem "The Ordinary Weather of Summer" could go like this:

"The Ordinary Weather of Summer"
Teacher's comment: The title suggests a sameness when the heat is always there, a kind of monotony of heat, yet summer also suggests life and fruitfulness and color, so a kind of tension is set up between monotony, or stagnation; and growth, or hope.

"In the ordinary weather of summer"
Teacher's Comment: Repeating the images from the title in the first line emphasizes the tension between ordinariness and summer-fullness, but now I am placed in the setting by the word *In*. It is an invitation to join an exploration and signals the beginning of a story.

"With storms rumbling from west to east"
Teacher's Comment: Now the air is electrically charged with the potential of storms. There is an ominousness that I feel from an image of clouds building and darkening and sounds of thunder, and yet the movement from west to east seems to also reinforce the ordinariness, as the storms recur

in the usual weather pattern. So I have an impression again of the tension between two forces, the expected and the turbulent.

WHY THIS WORKS: Cognitive modeling works because it:

1. Starts in a free association/brainstorming style that hooks into background experience and information.
2. Illustrates the mind's search for meaning as it produces tentative hypotheses, collects data, and refines hypotheses.
3. Naturally causes thought processes to surface: seeing images, noting feelings, exploring ideas, fixing up problems and contradictions, predicting outcomes, discovering questions, considering vocabulary cues, and anticipating meaning from titles.
4. Honestly reveals the uncertainties and tentativeness involved in the consideration of a new problem to be solved.
5. Builds confidence in students because they view an experienced thinker, the teacher, struggling with uncertainties and taking small steps toward solution making.
6. Builds confidence in students because they experience an open idea flow that aids them in analysis techniques.
7. Involves students subjectively in making meaning, thus creating more chance for learning.
8. Demonstrates reader response in an oral form.
9. Builds a broader base of information since students share thoughts with each other.
10. Suggests an approach to figuring out unfamiliar things.

(These ideas are adapted from a workshop on Cognitive Modeling by Jessie Lahr, Edison High School, Fairfax County, Virginia.)

## SOME SUGGESTED SOURCES FOR STORIES

Beck, M. L. 1990. *Heroes and Heroines: Tlingit-Haida Legend.* Anchorage: Alaska Northwest Books.

Blatt, G. T., ed. 1993. *Once upon a folktale: Capturing the folktale process with children*. New York: Teachers College Press.

Gunner, E. 1989. *A Handbook for Teaching African Literature: Second Edition*. Oxford: Heinemann International.

Masson, M. 1990. *A Bag of Bones: The Wintu Tales of a Trinity River Indian*. Happy Camp, Calif.: Naturegraph Company.

Mullet, G. M., ed. 1987. *Spider Woman Stories: Legends of the Hopi Indians*. Tucson: University of Arizona Press.

Sevillano, M., ed. 1986. *The Hopi Way: Tales from a Vanishing Culture*. Flagstaff, Ariz.: Northland Press.

Shipley, W., ed. 1991. *The Maidu Indian Myths and Stories of Hanc'ibyjim*. Berkeley: Heyday Books.

Stillman, P. R. 1985. *Introduction to Myth*. Portsmouth, N.H.: Boynton/Cook Publishers.

# • *Seven*

. . . . . . . . . . . . . . . .

## *Searching for Authentic Assessment*

When used in the singular to describe human accomplishment, a "standard" is an exemplary performance serving as a benchmark. . . . But there is no single model of excellence; there are always a variety of exemplars to emulate.　　　　　　　　　　　　　—*Wiggins*

*A*ssessment is here to stay. It makes sense to find out what is going on in the classroom. The problems associated with assessment arise because of its misapplication and misinterpretation. Teacher-proof standardized tests have little to do with the application of knowledge; they are designed for reliability, not validity. In addition, they generally measure lower-order thinking, are likely to favor a particular culture or gender, are used as negative rating systems, and are not linked to content instruction or the process of learning.

Assessment should be embedded in instructional practice and benefit both the learners and the teacher. Assessment, therefore, should be a continuous part of the learning process. The knowledge assessed should be worth the effort to learn it and the assessment techniques should reflect meaningful educational goals. Assessment should be "owned" by the students and the teacher. It is important to realize that assessments do not have to be uniform to be reasonable and responsible. Thoughtful instruments that reflect the quality of achievement can represent students with more validity than can standardized tests.

## *Valid Assessment*

The assessment of spoken language and listening presents hard questions to answer and harder ones to ask. Paper and pencil tests cannot assess a transactional event. Valid assessment of spoken language involves recognizing the complexity of the process. Just as excellent writing indicates excellent thinking, so also does excellent speaking. But what occurs enroute to those products? What means can be used to assess the process of thinking within speaking and listening? Since authentic learning should aim toward the goals of higher-order thinking, depth of knowledge, substantive dialogue, and the social support of achievement—assessment should not violate those goals. The reasoning process must be valued.

If we place excellence of product over excellence of process, we violate our goals. Leopold Mannes and Leopold Godowsky, who invented Kodachrome film, worked for twenty-four years to achieve the color film we take for granted. On that journey they had terrible failures. Assessment must include the efforts—the process of learning. Students need constant, careful, and consistent feedback—and a supportive atmosphere, one that says, "It's okay to make mistakes!"

The kinds of assessment that can support educational goals and students' efforts are those that are ongoing and flexible. Assessments should represent the different ways we "know." The problem, of course, is to set a standard for excellence on products and performances that are not at face value quantifiable. Andrew Stibbs (1980) provides a way to examine assessment graphically. Too often assessment is conceived of as measurement, when it can be profitably thought of as description as well. Describing behavior and progress can give a more detailed and inclusive picture of a child's accomplishments. The critieria we apply to our assessments should be flexible even as they are explicit.

> To apply criteria rigidly in assessment is inefficient teaching. Different uses of language call for the application of different criteria. . . . Silence can be good listening or poor talking. (p. 71)

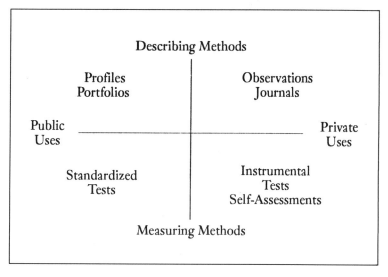

Figure 3: *Chart of Assessments (Stibbs 1980, 68)*

## Describing Methods

Stibbs visualizes assessments on a chart (see Figure 3). The profiles that appear in the top left quadrant can be derived in different ways. For instance, David Lazear (1992) suggests making an "Intelligence Profile" that would assess a student's use of the multiple intelligences identified by Howard Gardner (1991). Those seven intelligences are: verbal/linguistic, logical/mathematical, visual/spatial, body/kinesthetic, musical/rhythmic, interpersonal, and intrapersonal. This kind of profile is akin to a crossword puzzle. No one piece is the picture; it is only when all of the pieces fit together that the whole picture emerges. The profile is constructed as teachers observe students working on complex problems or creative inventions. They keep notes and checklists about behaviors to determine which forms of intelligence individuals prefer.

The teacher looks for answers to questions. Do students work alone or in groups? Do they ask questions? Do they move their bodies? Do they doodle? These descriptive profiles provide insight about speaking, writing, or thinking behaviors for regular or exceptional children. Profiles may be used publicly for placement, mainstream inclusion, diagnosis, or outside sources, such as probation officers. They also can shift to the upper right quadrant and become part of the teacher's own system of record keeping.

Portfolios also fall dually into both categories. They may be graded for public use by external standards, giving a "picture" of the child as a writer or thinker. Within the classroom, portfolios can be records that are mutually negotiated with a child in a private evaluation system.

Observations and journals, in the upper right quadrant, include anecdotes about students' progress and behavior. Learning logs and journals of both teachers and students belong here. The primary purposes are self-knowledge and classroom decisions about growth and progress. Self-questions, reflections, and pre- and post-lesson informal writings are some of the forms of assessment. Peer evaluations, videotapes, and informal discussions are other ways to gauge language learning.

## Measuring Methods

The lower right quadrant includes instrumental tests, informal evaluations of behaviors from checklists, and observations of learning behaviors. These can include student self-assessments on skills or learning styles. (A self-assessment checklist for communication apprehension can be found in Chapter 5. A sample listening self-assessment can be found in the Activities section of this chapter.) Teachers can use informal measurements to gauge students' abilities for many tasks:

1. Fluent reading
2. Fluent speaking
3. Selection and illustration of a poem
4. Use of supports for a claim
5. Location of main ideas

## Public Use versus Teacher Use

The current problem is that an overabundance of assessments come from the bottom left quadrant; too few come from the top half. Portfolios, one may recognize, are an effort to derive assessments from the other three quadrants for a more inclusive look at students' achievement. The problem with moving portfolios to the top left quadrant, public use, and reducing their assessment to numbers is that they lose their personal, anecdotal, and idiosyncratic value.

An additional problem with portfolio assessment, as it is usually described, is the sole reliance on writing samples to the exclusion of other forms of assessment, such as instrumentals or tapes. For example, the question teachers use to guide portfolio content standards in the California Assessment Collaborative (CAC) is: "What knowledge, skills, and habits in writing do you care about in students as readers, writers, listeners and speakers" (Flanagan 1993, 2)? However, writing is not the best way to assess speaking. If actual tapes cannot be included in the portfolios, peer evaluations, self-assessments, and other instrumentals can indicate progress in speaking and listening.

## Counterproductive Standards

Demands for rigorous standards and high achievement for all students resonate well in the press, but their effect in the classroom can be otherwise. Strict adherence to performance standards and accuracy in speaking, writing, and reading can be counterproductive: stunting language development, inhibiting fluent talk, and forestalling ambitious writing or better reading (Stibbs 1980). Teachers have to help students learn to value their own process and efforts more than our marks on their products. They have to learn that improvement can be cooperatively achieved, and true learning comes about when they can self-assess and correct their own mistakes, often with the help of others, and sometimes on their own.

We as teachers have to value our own observations and judgments. We have to learn to record field notes and keep self-made checklists. And when a child shows enthusiasm for reading, eagerly finishing one book and looking for another by the same author, we have to recognize that we are probably seeing a better indication of reading ability than a normed score. When a child begins to share ideas in a small group, we may be seeing a better indication of that child's progress in oral communication than from a semi-annual oral book report. Frank Smith (1989) also warns against an overemphasis on testing. "I have never seen evidence that testing produces literacy—though there are massive indications that it has the opposite effect" (p. 356).

## Oral Process Assessment

The process of speaking and listening presents its own special problem with assessment. In writing, when we assess process, it is the individual's writing that we are looking at. In oral communication, we have a dynamic, transitory situation involving the individual and an audience. The oral performance may have certain standards based upon set expectations, but what about discussion? Group dynamics, the task, and setting affect individuals' contributions. If students build on each other's ideas, they may not articulate complete statements (Stables 1992). Those students who present longer, more complete thought units, may negatively affect others, causing them to participate less. How do we evaluate supportive nonverbal behaviors, such as smiling and eye contact?

If we value English as a process rather than a product subject, then we must design an array of experiences and assessments that capture the oral components of language. One oral presentation, or even two, does not tell the story, nor does one group discussion, regardless of whether the student is an active or reticent participant. Different group companions, different tasks, and different situations will affect the competence of the individuals. Think of yourself in three types of groups—a meeting with national leaders, a group of parents, or a Neighborhood Watch organizational meeting. How actively would you speak and listen in each of the settings? Certainly, your behavior would alter based on the circumstances. So do children's.

In addition, a small group does not operate the same way when it is observed as it does unobserved, although a tape recorder may allow a more natural kind of interaction. Individual students show marked differences in behavior between small group peer discussions and those with the whole class, whether the teacher leads those discussions or not (O'Keefe 1988b). This means that we have to involve students in more self-assessment, since our very presence as teachers colors their performance.

Communication is situation-specific and does not thrive in a climate of evaluation. Oral communication evaluation, especially, is most likely to create anxiety and artificial behaviors. Those individuals who experience extreme communication apprehension (see a description in Chapter 5) will suffer the most in an evaluative situation. For that reason teachers should exercise caution when they assess children's oral communication.

## Alternative Assessment

Testing and evaluative methods that can create anxiety and camouflage actual competence should be replaced or reduced by assessment processes that are more inclusive and more reflective of actual performance. Such a transition is not easy. Not the least of the problems is that alternative methods are time-consuming to establish, maintain, and evaluate. For instance, a short essay written in response to a standard prompt, when graded by set criteria, takes on average between ten to fifteen minutes to grade. Multiply that time by 135 students, or the average teacher's roll, and we have approximately twenty-two to thirty-four hours devoted to a piece of writing, for no other purpose than to assess a pupil's standing.

Add to that marking time the hours spent in establishing the criteria and achieving grading consistency among teachers, if it is a departmental effort. No wonder attempts such as these, which look good on paper, are short-lived and die in their own red ink. Nevertheless, there is an explosion of interest in alternative assessment and a similar eruption of suggestions for their creation without real guidance from national or state governments clamoring for more accountability (Herman, Aschbacher, and Winters 1992).

Alternative assessment is considered synonymous with "authentic assessment" and "performance-based assessment." Their commonality is that they require students to generate rather than choose a response. Alternative assessment can take many forms:

Exhibitions
Investigations
Demonstrations
Written or oral responses
Conferencing
Sharing
Projects
Group interviews
Artifacts
Videotapes or audiotapes
Learning logs/journals
Self-evaluations
Inventories/surveys
Behavioral checklists/observations
Peer assessment
Portfolios

This is only a partial list. The creative teacher and student can think of many more. Alternative assessments ideally test the process as well as the product of learning, with greater emphasis on becoming a learner. An interesting or complex task by itself does not guarantee a good assessment. The results of a good assessment should inform both the students and the teacher what has been accomplished. The students' participation in the goal of assessment is a crucial factor. Their coparticipation can remove the anxiety and return ownership to them even for the evaluation stage of learning. As a concrete example, the writing process demonstrates this validity. Students work with peers and with the teacher-coach through a series of stages to improve writing. The final grade reflects those steps, those efforts, and those revisions.

## Meaningful Assessment

How, then, can speaking, listening, and thinking be assessed in meaningful ways? Apparently the oral performance, a popular speaking assignment, has surfaced along with forms of writing as an "alternative assessment." No shortage of evaluation models exist; some are included in the Activities section of this chapter. The problem with most of them is that they are too complex and demanding. Students are judged on content, organization, transitions, word choice, style of delivery, posture, eye contact, and vocal quality. This format is even more stringent than our requirement for writing. Unfortunately, in speech we tend to grade heavily what might be called "punctuation." After all, with writing we usually allow revision. A speech is all or nothing, a onetime event.

How might performance be graded more equitably? Instead of one assignment fulfilling multiple criteria, we could have several assignments each fulfilling a separate criteria, with perhaps the final one encompassing all. Records of these talks would become part of the child's portfolio, with comments and responses by peers, teacher, and the child about the experiences. When a dozen or more assignments are involved, we would hope that the child would be able to pick topics close to her interest and experience as she would with writing. We would also hope that the frequency and informality of the talks would increase both her competency and fluency. Perhaps we could remove that terror of speaking that infects at least 20 percent of our population.

The first priority for all speaking performances should be to develop a fluency of language about real content. Writers write about real subjects that matter to them for real audiences. A speaker has an audience, all right, but if that audience is counting her "umms" instead of listening to her story, I doubt that it is "real." Couple that artificiality with a contrived subject, the book report, and we have a speaking situation designed for schoolese, not the real world.

Just as we learned that red markings all over a child's writing inhibit writing, red marking a child's speech has the same deleterious effect. Even more personal than writing, speaking performance is treated as an object to be graded, forgetting the red-faced child standing behind those words. These two practices in the average classroom devalue both speaking and the student speaker.

## Authentic Communication Assessment

Instead, assessment of communication should be ongoing by the students and teacher. For instance, every communication event has a listening component. Students can learn to listen and respond to discussions, performances, and readings. These listening responses become part of the evaluation process. Students as they prepare reports and projects can share and revise their presentations in groups. Before oral performances, dyads can practice for each other, refining word choice and organizational patterns. These activities are all part of an evaluative process without penalty. The same kind of cooperative atmosphere that has helped to improve writing can also improve speaking and listening, with dramatic results.

### Peer Assessment

Giving students the responsibility for listening and responding to their peers teaches two things: how to listen better, and how to prepare better. Individuals can respond singly or as groups. One method that has worked quite well at the secondary and college level is to assign panels to listen to performances. Their job is not just to summarize the material presented, but to construct challenging questions for the speakers. Was the evidence sufficient for the conclusion? What kind of evidence is offered as proof? Has the problem been probed sufficiently? What information was omitted? Are the sources cited accurately? Generating questions forces students to think about the material and not just accept information as it is presented. Questions help the speakers to probe their topics more thoroughly.

These kinds of activities can be done as preparation for the big day in front of the class. Or they can be part of the oral performance event itself. Samples of peer evaluation forms are included in the Activity section at the end of this chapter.

## Self-Assessment

Self-assessment may be at the heart of the performance assessment movement and can take many forms. After peer assessments, students can write reflections about what they learned from their classmates' comments. "Perhaps the most powerful tool a student can use is a journal" (Marzano, Pickering, McTighe 1994, 35). Students can use checklists about their perceptions of themselves as listeners, their learning styles, or other factors that influence communication or learning. Informal writings about texts, observations, and reactions to the business of the classroom are all forms of self-assessment. Self-assessment gives ownership of the learning situation to the child and helps to influence her or his abilities to use metacognition, or thinking about thinking. Ashley, a graduate education student, struggles with this idea in her journal:

> What I have discovered through my "thinking journal" is that although my approach is logical and systematic, what happens inside my head is beyond understanding. When I begin a paper, I collect all the information I can find. I read everything and "input" the data. It is almost like I am programming my mind. I think about what I have put into my brain at random intervals for varying amounts of time and then sit down at the computer.

I often find myself thinking about my paper in the middle of the night or at off times. Whatever, when I sit down, "the knowledge" just kind of spills out. Does that sound weird? I have never thought about my thinking processes before and just assumed everyone else was like me. But after studying thinking, I wonder. Am I different in my thinking processes? Is my process that of a scientist or an artist? There is some of both, I think.

## Journals

Journals and learning logs are valuable at any point in the learning process. Students in a college introductory interpersonal communication class wrote journals about their reactions to some of the theories and studies mentioned in the course. Sabrina questions the findings in one study:

In a 1987 study by Yogev, the results were that spouses were more happy in their marriages if they perceived that their spouses fit the sex-role stereotypes. I know there is a segment of the American population that sees that this result of Yogev's study is true. But I also know that some people approve of the fact that Hillary Rodham Clinton is a strong and independent woman and that her husband, President Bill Clinton, asked her to work on the health care plan for this country. Hillary Rodham Clinton doesn't fit the usual role of First Lady and some people are supporting her for being a strong and independent woman.

Translating theories, texts, and classroom activities into the students' own words places these events into their constructs. It allows them to test ideas and to concretize abstractions. Yuka writes about the differences in cross-cultural communication:

Living in America requires me to be more assertive than being in my home country. Here, I have to state clearly and directly what I want and what I do not want, otherwise, nobody will sense my feeling and do it for me. Where I come from, I do not have to be as assertive as I have to be here, and people would understand what I am implying. For example, when I say, "I have a lot of study tonight. I have a big test tomorrow," to my roommate, I am implying to her that I do not want TV on or do not want her to talk on the phone in a loud voice. If she does not get it, she can be seen as a inconsiderate individual in my culture. However, that is not the case in American culture, I have understood. Probably she would say, "Well, you did not tell me you wanted TV off."

Secondary students also can write responses to literature during the process of reading. These informal writings become the springboards for discussion. Natalie writes:

As I continue to read *Heart of the Matter*, by Graham Greene, I seem to have more and more questions about the characters. There is one character in particular who boggles my mind, and that character is Scobie. One question which has been bothering me is why is he referred to as Ticki? I assumed that one of these two is his real name and the other is a nickname, but I don't know which one. I am hoping my reading group will help me with this. This may seem trivial, but when you're reading a book, at times two names, when referring to one person, can get quite confusing.

## Portfolios

Interestingly, all the forms of assessment discussed above can find their way into the portfolio. There is nothing new about collecting students' work. In the past, as Christine Sobrey Evans (1993, 71), a classroom teacher, observed:

The portfolios were organized storage bins, where work went in but never came out. Then at the end of the year, the portfolios were sent home—much like a scrapbook for the year.

Portfolios are different. Students select their best work, or work that represents their best effort. These collections become part of the evaluation system. Portfolio content is discipline and purpose specific. In graduate education school, it might consist of research, projects, model lessons, observations, and teaching-learning-logs. For the in-service teacher it might be a collection of published articles, evidence of community work, samples of student writing, and field notes on student progress. A secondary student's portfolio might have journals, project descriptions, discussion and performance evaluations, illustrations of literature, creative writing, interview reports, listener or observer responses, peer evaluations and self-assessments of listening and speaking. Sometimes colleges require students to prepare portfolios to demonstrate critical thinking abilities (Aiken and Neer 1992). Portfolios can contain products of completed projects, artifacts, incomplete projects, tests, and ideas for new projects (Marzano 1992). While portfolios are not limited to writing, informal journals may be the most valuable part.

The advantage of portfolios is that they are an inclusive form of assessment. They allow an interaction between the students and the teacher that can be a nonevaluative form of assessment. Teachers can respond to student work and questions in an ongoing dialogue. This form of interaction becomes a sort of coaching. Luke answers a teacher's comment to his journal:

> After reading [the comment sheet] it got me thinking about what I wrote about and how narrow my thinking had been while writing the journal. After the fact being pointed out to me, I realized how many cross-cultural and intimate contacts, for example, that I actually have every day. I never realized the extent to which little boys, for example, connect with older role models, especially if they share the same interests.

But the real value in portfolios is not for the outside agency, or even better assessment by a department, it is for the classroom teacher who gains valuable insights into her students' thoughts.

## Assessment and the Classroom Teacher

Inclusive, multifaceted, and varied forms of assessment give the teacher valuable information about her students. Learning to trust her judgment is an important step in the professionalism of our discipline. Documenting what occurs helps us to improve our practice and builds the kind of research to show a

connection between teaching and student behavior. Reliability
in the scoring of portfolios, or any other form of assessment, is
less meaningful than the validity of seeing and hearing the
voices of the students as represented through their accumu-
lated efforts. An excerpt from Michael's journal about his
problems and learnings in a communication class illustrate this
kind of growth with a particular poignancy.

As I opened the long awaited [catalog of classes], many thoughts
were floating through my head. I knew I would have to take a
class in communication because my major required me to. A class
I needed but always avoided if possible, dating back to high
school. Communication, you see, was not my strong point. In
fact, I almost dreaded it. My immediate reaction was, "I hope
this class is going to help me overcome my shyness!" So, when
told we must find a question which we would answer every week
in a journal entry by relating the chapters of the week to it, I had
an easy time because the same question ran through my head.
How is this course in communication going to help me overcome
my shyness around strangers? People I haven't known long and
don't quite feel comfortable around. I came in with basically
what I consider no communication skills whatsoever. I would
discover this to be wrong later on, but there was no doubt that I
needed help.

It seems as though communication starts with yourself. With
this being the case, problems started for me right there. How you
view yourself and the others around you has an impact on the
way you communicate. As I said in the very first journal, "I have
very low self-esteem and oftentimes, I am worried about what
others think of me." If you don't think highly of yourself at all,
then communication will be a hard and painful process for you. I
worry about what others think of me. Probably too much as a
matter of fact. . . . It hurts to think people don't want to talk to
you, so sooner or later, you will pretend you are doing them a
favor and you won't talk to them. Once the talking begins,
though, it doesn't get any better. I am one of those people you
talk to but you can't really hear what they are saying because
they talk so lightly. Conversation is really hard because it is a
two way street and both parties must want something out of it.

Otherwise it is almost useless. Speaking is only part of communication, though, the hard part if you ask me. It was the part I
needed to work on the most, and the part I feel was helped the
most by taking a communication class . . . Everything I described
earlier was me, but as I sit here and think to myself, I realize that
was the old me. It was the me that lived off in my own world.
Content knowing the people I knew, but still always worrying
about what everyone else thought. The me that was too shy to talk
to others, to participate in class, and to show people who I really
was. That was the old me. The new me is willing to talk, not only
listen. The new person who is growing to like himself, which as
we all know, is the first step in successful communication. Only
time can tell if I will someday be a good communicator, but the
base is there and it is up to me to continue to grow as a person. I
must not forget what I have been taught, instead, I must expand
on it so that someday the new me will become the ultimate me.

How many Michaels do we have in our classes? One out of
five, or possibly more. Young people have been intimidated by
our overemphasis on the wrong values in speech. It is true, we
can avoid speech assignments by concentrating on writing, but
that only begs the issue. The Michaels and the Yukas in our
classes need to practice speaking and listening in a supportive
atmosphere. Our job is to build their skills, not to red mark
their attempts. Language development is more than reading
and writing. Speech is basic to all learning.

## World-Class Standards

World-class standards of education must be established if our
children are to be truly competitive in the world of the twenty-
first century. Higher goals are realistic for most students, not
just the elite. The question we must answer is how to achieve
those goals without some kind of rigid, "standardized" form
of assessment. What we must remember is that meaning is
constructed and that knowledge, to be authentic, requires
a change in the individual. We "become" as we learn. As a

community of learners, inquiry-based instruction will enrich us all, teachers and students. The potential is there, but will we have the courage to tap it? Will we have the courage to speak up effectively? The silent classroom is not healthy for students' self-concepts nor for their intellectual development. Silent teachers are even more devastating, because in silence we lose both our own voices and those of our students.

*Teacher-Researcher Questions*

1. What kinds of observations of students' behaviors would be useful to determine their awareness of interpersonal communication skills?
2. How can teacher journals be used to gauge individual students' progress in communication?
3. How might portfolio design provide a more inclusive picture of students for the classroom teacher?
4. How might oral communication be evaluated so that students can benefit from more authentic assessment methods?

## • *ACTIVITIES* •

### PEER EVALUATIONS

OBJECTIVE: Students learn to evaluate by performance objectives when they must observe and assess classmates using specific criteria. Having a responsibility to complete a written evaluation emphasizes the role of the listener. The evaluation forms also clarify performance objectives for students when it is their turn to become the speaker.

PROCESS:

1. Students are assigned certain speakers to evaluate and to question.
2. Hand out one of the following forms, or an adaptation depending on the assignment.

3. When an individual speaker (or several) has completed an assignment, the listeners give oral critiques, ask questions, or make positive comments about the content and/or the delivery.
4. The listeners can form panels and share the task of responding to the speeches and speakers.
5. After giving speeches on a particular day, the speakers can be placed in different parts of the room. Those listeners who wrote their critiques can meet and talk with them in small groups.
6. Collect the listener forms. Credit the listener with points. Give the written critiques to the speakers along with the teacher's evaluation. Student evaluations usually positively reinforce the teacher's remarks.

WHY THIS WORKS: Students practice the responsibilities of both listener and speaker when there is a specific task to accomplish as a listener. As speakers they appreciate the feedback from their peers, just as we have encouraged feedback in writing groups.

---

*Panel Analysis of Argument Speech*

---

Name: _____ Date: _____

Speaker: _____

Topic/Argument: _____

Argument Structure
    Major conclusion:
    Types of arguments:
    Reasons:
    Support included (sufficient evidence, credible sources):
    Validity of authorities (expert, lay):

Content
    Use of sources:
    Sources cited in speech:

Substantive information:
Examples:

Questions:

Evaluation:

---

*Listener Report: Argument Speech*

Name: _____ Date: _____

Speaker: _____

Topic/Argument: _____

Argument analysis:
　Major conclusions:
　Support:
　Evidence:

Your question:

---

*Listener Report: Informative Speech with Visual Aid*

Name: _____ Date: _____

Speaker: _____

Content:
　Was topic worthwhile?
　Were four sources cited?
　Were major ideas supported with examples?
　Was visual used effectively?

Organization:
　Was time limit of six to eight minutes observed?
　Did key topics follow an outline?
　Was introduction clear?
　Was body of speech structured logically?
　Did conclusion summarize?

Delivery:
> Was eye contact maintained?
> Was speech delivered from notes?
> Was speech practiced?
> Was delivery fluent?

---

### *Observer Form: Small Group Problem Analysis*

---

This form is designed for observers as they watch a small group analyze a problem. The emphasis is on content as well as the group members' interaction. The observers do not give points for the discussion. Their task is to give specific feedback to the participants.

Group Members: _____

Topic: _____

Content: After this discussion, I have learned the following ideas about the problem:
> The problem is identified as:
> Possible causes are:
> Obstacles, current policies, and solutions are:

Process: During this presentation, I observed the following speaking and listening behaviors that contributed to an effective discussion:

During this presentation, I observed the following task and maintenance functions that contributed to an effective discussion:

During this presentation, I observed the following leadership functions that contributed to an effective discussion:

Product: Overall, this group's presentation was effective because:

Overall, this group's presentation could have been improved if they:

## SPEECH EVALUATION FORMS

The speech evaluation forms that follow are intended to encourage the writing of comments to the speakers instead of just giving points for performance. They can be used by the teacher or peers.

*News Item Speech Evaluation*

Name: _____ Date: _____

Topic: _____

1. Student is prepared with article from magazine or newspaper.

5 _____

2. Student explains article and the main ideas.        10 _____

3. Student presents his/her opinion about the subject
with reasons.        15 _____

Comments:

*Impromptu Speech Evaluation*

Name: _____ Date: _____

Subject: _____ Time: _____

Objective: To speak in a fluent, organized manner on an impromptu subject. The time for the speech is one to three minutes. The method may be anecdotal (telling a story) or expository (explaining), but the speech should make a point and have a beginning, middle, and end.

1. Speech content (main points):

2. Speech organization (chronological or topical):

3. Interest to audience (How did it relate to audience?):

4. Delivery:

5. General suggestions for improvement:

Evaluator:

---

## *Oral Presentation Evaluation*

Name: _____ Date: _____

Visual Type: _____

Subject: _____

Content: The student explains a subject, demonstrating her or his use of research. The talk should be planned and contain factual material. The visual should be explained in relation to the topic.

| | |
|---|---|
| Clarity of message | 5 Points |
| Content (examples, facts) | 5 Points |
| Depth of understanding | 5 Points |

Comments:


Delivery: The student is poised when addressing the audience. The student should stand with weight on both feet, have eye contact, and speak with sufficient volume and rate to be understood by the class.

| | |
|---|---|
| Eye contact and poise | 5 Points |
| Vocal control | 5 Points |
| | Total 25 Points |

Comments:

## SELF-ASSESSMENT

OBJECTIVE: Students learn to self-assess their behaviors. These forms should not be "graded." In order to improve we have to become aware of our strengths and weaknesses.

PROCESS:

1. Self-assessments can be teacher administered, as is the Listening Assessment. Or they can be self-reports such as the Listening Action Plan or Small Group Participation Report.
2. These assessment forms should become part of the total progress evaluation of a student. Students should keep these materials in their portfolios as a reference for themselves and a diagnostic tool for the teacher.

WHY THIS WORKS: Students can understand their own progress and their own responsibility in the process of learning. Instead of the prescriptions for behaviors all originating from the adult in the classroom, students learn to self-evaluate their progress and develop goals for improvement.

*Listening Assessment*

Instructor: I want you to challenge yourselves to listen as you have never listened before. I will share a fifty-eight-word message with you and then ask you some questions about the content of the message.

*Assessment Message:*
　　The owner of the Johnson Industrial Company entered the office of one of his supervisors, where he found three employees playing cards. One of them was Jeff Adams, brother-in-law of supervisor Bill Fleming. Fleming, incidentally, often worked late. Company rules did not specifically forbid gambling on the premises, but the president had expressed himself forcibly on the subject.

Instructor: I'm going to make twelve statements about the message. You are to label each statement as TRUE, FALSE, or

*173*

Question Mark (?). Base your answers on the information provided in the message. Write TRUE if the statement is true. Write FALSE if the statement is false. Write a question mark if the statement is questionable; that is, if not enough information was provided for you to determine if the statement is true or false.

### Questions (with Answer Key)

Read questions and read answers (given in parentheses) afterwards. Have students tabulate their scores. Calculate the class' mean average of correct answers. Show students a transparency of the Assessment Message as you go over each statement and answer.

1. In brief, the message is about a company owner who found three men playing cards. (?)
2. The president entered the office of one of his supervisors. (?)
3. Company rules forbade card playing on the premises after hours. (?)
4. While card-playing took place in Bill Fleming's office, the message does not state whether or not Fleming was present. (?)
5. Fleming never worked late. (FALSE)
6. Gambling on the premises of the Johnson Industrial Company was not punished. (?)
7. Jeff Adams was not playing cards when the president entered. (?)
8. Three employees were gambling in a supervisor's office. (?)
9. While the card players were surprised when the owner entered, it is not clear whether or not they were punished. (?)
10. Bill Fleming was Jeff Adams' brother-in-law. (TRUE)
11. Jeff Adams did not take part in the card game in Bill Fleming's office. (?)
12. A corporation owner found three employees playing cards. (?)

(From Coakley, Carolyn. 1993. *Teaching Effective Listening: A Practical Guide for the High School Classroom.* New Orleans: Spectra, Inc., 78–79)

### Listening Action Plan

Instructions: Begin now to create an action plan for improving your listening behavior. Throughout this course, continue to add to your action plan. In your plan, include the following:

1. Your strengths as a listener
2. Your weaknesses as a listener
3. Your action plan to improve your listening weaknesses
4. Your means of determining how successful you are in improving your listening weaknesses

Use the following format for your action plan:

My listening strengths:
 1.
 2.
 3.

My listening weaknesses:
 1.
 2.
 3.

My action plan for improving my listening weaknesses:
 1.
 2.
 3.

My means of determining my success in improving my listening weaknesses:
 1.
 2.
 3.

(From Coakley, Carolyn. 1993. *Teaching Effective Listening: A Practical Guide for the High School Classroom*. New Orleans: Spectra, Inc., 80.)

*Report on Individual Participation in Small Group Activity*

Name: _____

Group Members: _____

For this presentation I contributed the following:
 1.
 2.

3.

4.

For this presentation I prepared the following (Put your name on any materials you helped with):

1.

2.

3.

4.

I spent this amount of time on the project:

Date                        Amount of Time                        Task


My most valuable contribution to the group was:

The most important thing(s) that I learned was (were):

Comments:


## SOURCES FOR INFORMATION ABOUT SPEAKING
## AND LISTENING ACTIVITIES AND ASSESSMENTS

The following speaking and listening competency materials are available from Speech Communication Association (SCA), 5105 Backlick Rd., Building E, Annandale, VA 22003.

- Cooper, P. 1985. *Activities for Teaching Speaking and Listening: Grades 7–12.*
- Daniel, A. V. 1992. *Activities Integrating Oral Communication Skills for Students Grades K–8.*
- *Speaking and Listening Competencies*, 1994.

# References

Adler, M. 1983. *How to speak: How to listen.* N.Y.: Macmillan.

Adler, R. B., and G. Rodman. 1991. *Understanding human communication.* Orlando, Fla: Holt, Rinehart, and Winston, Inc.

Aiken, J. E., and M. Neer. 1992. A faculty program of assessment for a college level competency-based communication core curriculum. *Communication Education* 41(3): 270–286.

Applebee, A. N. 1978. *The child's concept of story.* Chicago: University of Chicago Press.

Applebee, A. N., and J. A. Langer. 1984. Instructional scaffolding: Reading and writing as natural language activities. Pp. 183–190 in *Composing and comprehending.* Edited by J. M. Jensen. Urbana, Ill.: ERIC/Educational Resources Information Center Clearinghouse on Reading and Communication Skills.

Barnes, D. 1976. Language strategies in learning. In *Classroom encounters.* Edited by M. Torbe. London: National Association for Teachers of English.

———. 1990. Oral language and learning. In *Perspectives on talk and learning.* Edited by S. Hynds and D. L. Rubin. Urbana, Ill.: National Council of Teachers of English (NCTE).

Bernstein, B. 1971. *Class, codes and control.* Vol 1. London: Routledge and Kegan Paul.

Bloom, B. S., ed. 1979. *Taxonomy of educational objectives: Book 1 Cognitive domain.* London: Longman Group Ltd.

Brilhart, J. K., and G. J. Galanes. 1989. *Effective group discussion.* 6th ed. Dubuque, Iowa: Wm. C. Brown.

Britton, J. 1970. *Language and learning.* London: Penguin Books, Ltd.

———. 1982. In *Prospect and retrospect: Selected essays of James Britton.* Edited by G. M. Pradl. Upper Montclair, N.J.: Boynton/Cook Publishers, Inc.

Bruner, J. 1973. In *Beyond the information given: Studies in the psychology of knowing.* Edited by J. M. Anglin. New York: W. W. Norton & Company, Inc.

Chase, N. D., and C. R. Hynd. 1987. Reader response: An alternate way to teach students to think about text. *Journal of Reading* 30 (March): 530–540.

Christenbury, L., and P. R. Kelly. 1983. *Questioning a path to critical thinking.* Urbana, Ill.: ERIC/National Council of Teachers of English (NCTE).

Ciardi, J., and M. Williams. 1975. *How does a poem mean?* Boston: Houghton Mifflin Company.

Coakley, C. 1993. *Teaching effective listening: A practical guide for the high school classroom.* New Orleans: Spectra, Inc.

Cohen, E. G., and J. Benton. 1988. Making groupwork work. *American Educator* 12(3): 10–17.

Cooper, P. J. 1990. *Activities for teaching speaking and listening: Grades 7–12.* Annandale, Va.: Speech Communication Association, ERIC.

———. 1995. *Speech communication for the classroom teacher.* 5th ed. Scottsdale, Ariz.: Gorsuch Scarisbrick, Publishers.

Cornbleth, C., speaker. 1976. *Students questioning and learning.* Fair Lawn, N.J.: Jab Press. Sound cassette No. 415.

Dahl, R. 1985. The landlady. Pp. 822–827 in *English literature.* Edited by R. C. Granner and M. E. Stern. Evanston, Ill.: McDougal, Littell & Company.

*Education research report.* 1992. Office of Educational Research and Improvement, U.S. Department of Education.

Elkind, D. 1981. *Children and Adolescents: Interpretive Essays on Jean Piaget.* Oxford: Oxford University Press.

Escalante, J. 1993. Speaking for education. *Virginia Journal of Education* 86 (2): 2.

Evans, C. S. 1993. When teachers look at student work. *Educational Leadership* 50 (5): 71–72.

Feezel, J. D. 1989. Teacher questions as students hear them. *Teacher Talk* 7 (1): 3.

Fish, S. 1980. *Is there a text in this class? The authority of interpretive communities.* Cambridge: Harvard University Press.

Fisher, B. A. 1974. *Small group decision making.* New York: McGraw-Hill Book Company.

Flanagan, A. 1993. New standards take a close look at portfolios. *The Council Chronicle* 3 (2): 1–3.

Frye, P. A. 1992. Quiz bowl: A check for daily reading. *The Speech Communication Teacher: Ideas and Strategies for Classrooms and Activities* 7 (1): 7.

Gardner, H. 1985. *The mind's new science: A history of the cognitive revolution.* New York: Basic Books, Inc.

Gersten, R., and J. Dimino. 1989. Teaching literature to at-risk students. *Educational Leadership* 46 (5, February): 53–57.

Good, T. L., and J. E. Brophy. 1991. *Looking in classrooms.* 5th ed. New York: HarperCollins Publishers, Inc.

Goodman, K., and Y. Goodman. 1984. Reading and writing relationships: Pragmatic functions. Pp. 155–164 in *Composing and comprehending.* Edited by J. M. Jensen. Urbana, Ill.: ERIC/Educational Resources Information Center Clearinghouse on Reading and Communication Skills.

*Guidelines for developing oral communication curricula in kindergarten through twelfth grade.* 1991. Annandale, Va.: Speech Communication Association.

Herman, J. L., P. R. Aschbacher, and L. Winters. 1992. *A practical guide to alternative assessment.* Alexandria, Va.: Association for Supervision and Curriculum Development.

Holbrook, H. T. 1987. Reader response to the classroom. *Journal of Reading* 30 (March): 556–559.

Iser, W. 1974. *The implied reader.* Baltimore and London: The Johns Hopkins University Press.

Johnson, D. W., and Johnson, R. T. 1989–1990. Social skills for successful group work. *Educational Leadership* 47 (4), 30.

————. 1991. Collaboration and cognition. Pp. 298–301 in *Developing minds: A Resource book for teaching thinking*. Rev. ed. Vol. 1. Edited by A. L. Costa. Alexandria, Va.: Association for Supervision and Curriculum Development.

Jones, B. F., A. S. Pallincsar, D. S. Ogle, and E. G. Carr. 1987. *Strategic teaching and learning: Cognitive instruction in the content areas*. Alexandria, Va.: Association for Supervision and Curriculum Development.

King, S. 1988. The nature of communication. Pp. 250–259 in *Small group communication: A reader*. 5th ed. Edited by R. S. Cathcart and L. S. Samovar. Dubuque, Iowa: Wm. C. Brown Publishers.

Lazear, D. G. 1992. *Teaching for multiple intelligences*. Bloomington, Ind.: Phi Delta Kappa Educational Foundation.

Loban, W. 1976. *Language development: Kindergarten through grade twelve*. Illinois: National Council of Teachers of English.

Martin, N., ed. 1976. *Writing across the curriculum*. Upper Montclair, N.J.: Boynton/Cook Publishers, Inc.

Marzano, R. J. 1992. *A different kind of classroom: Teaching with dimensions of learning*. Alexandria, Va.: Association for Supervision and Curriculum Development.

Marzano, R. J., D. Pickering, and J. McTighe. 1994. *Assessing student outcomes: Performance assesssment using dimensions of learning model*. Alexandria, Va.: Association for Supervision and Curriculum Development.

McCaleb, J. L. 1989. Escape from trivial pursuits: Evaluating teachers' communications. In *The future of speech communication*. Edited by P. J. Cooper and K. M. Galvin. Annandale, Va.: Speech Communication Association.

McCroskey, J. C., and V. P. Richmond. 1988. Communication apprehension and small group communication. Pp. 405–420 in *Small group communication: A reader*. 5th ed. Edited by R. S. Cathcart and L. S. Samovar. Dubuque, Iowa: Wm. C. Brown Publishers.

————. 1991. *Quiet children and the classroom teacher*. Annandale, Va.: Speech Communication Association and ERIC/Educational Resources Information Center.

Moffett, J. 1968. *Teaching the universe of discourse*. Boston: Houghton Mifflin Company.

National Assessment of Educational Progress. 1981, October. *Reading, thinking, and writing: Results from the 1979–1980 national assessment of reading and literature*. Denver, Colo.: Education Commission of the States.

O'Keefe, V. P. 1988a. *Affecting critical thinking through speech*. Urbana, Ill.: ERIC/Educational Resources Information Center Clearinghouse on Reading and Communication Skills.

————. 1988b. Student discourse in a secondary English class: A descriptive case study of the connections between speaking and writing activities and understanding of a literary text. *Dissertation Abstracts International*. (University Microfilms, No. 8825256).

————. 1992. Review essay: Intermediate and secondary level textbooks in speech communication. *Communication Education* 41 (4): 440–451.

Parker, R. P., and V. Goodkin. 1987. *The consequences of writing: Enhancing learning in the disciplines*. Upper Montclair, N.J.: Boynton/Cook Publishers, Inc.

Pastan, L. 1988. *The ordinary weather of summer. The imperfect paradise*. New York: W. W. Norton and Company, p. 44.

Paul, R. 1993. *Critical thinking: How to prepare students for a rapidly changing world*. Santa Rosa, Calif.: Foundation for Critical Thinking.

Perkins, D. 1992. *Smart schools: From training memories to training minds*. New York: The Free Press.

Piaget, J., and B. Inhelder. 1966. *The psychology of the child*. London: Routledge and Kegan Paul.

Postman, N., and C. Weingartner. 1969. *Teaching as a subversive activity*. New York: Delta.

Resnick, L. B., and Klopfer, L. E. 1989. Toward the thinking curriculum: An overview. In *Toward the thinking curriculum: Current cognitive research*. Edited by L. B. Resnick and L. E. Klopfer. Alexandria, Va.: Association for Supervision and Curriculum Development.

Richards, I. A. 1929. *Practical criticism: A study of literary judgement*. San Diego: Harcourt Brace Jovanovich Publishers.

Rogers, T., J. L. Green, J. F. Nussbaum, and N. Ryan. 1990. Asking questions about questions. In *Perspectives on talk and learning*. Edited by S. Hynds and D. L. Rubin. Urbana, Ill.: National Council of Teachers of English (NCTE).

Rosenblatt, L. M. 1978. *The reader, the text, the poem*. Carbondale, Ill.: Southern Illinois University Press.

Rowe, M. B. 1986. Wait times: Slowing down may be a way of speeding up! *Journal of Teacher Education* 37(1): 43–50.

Rubin, R., and S. A. Henzl. 1984. Cognitive complexity, communication competence, and verbal ability. *Communication Quarterly* 32 (4): 263–270.

*SCA guidelines: Essential speaking and listening skills for elementary school students (6th grade level)*. 1984. Annandale, Va.: Speech Communication Association.

*SCA guidelines: Speaking and listening competencies for high school graduates*. 1987. Annandale, Va.: Speech Communication Association.

Shakespeare, W. Sonnet 141. In *The complete works of William Shakespeare*. Vol. 2. Edited by W. G. Clark and W. A. Wright. Garden City, N.Y.: Nelson Doubleday, Inc.

Smagorinsky, P., and P. K. Fly. 1993. The social environment of the classroom: A Vygotskian perspective on small group process. *Communication Education* 42(2): 159–171.

Smith, F. 1989. Overselling literacy, *Phi Delta Kappan*. (January) 353–370.

———. 1990. *To think*. New York: Teachers College Press.

Sommer, R. 1969. *Personal space: The behavior basis of design*. Englewood Cliffs, N.J.: Prentice Hall, p. 118.

Sommer, R., and H. Olsen. 1980. The soft classroom. *Environment and behavior* 12 (March): 3–16.

Stables, A. 1992. Speaking and listening at key stages 3: Some summary problems of teacher assessment. *Educational Research* 34 (2): 107–115.

Stibbs, A. 1980. *Assessing children's language: Guidelines for teachers*. London: Ward Lock Educational.

Stubbs, M. 1976. *Language, schools, and classrooms*. London: Methuen & Co. Ltd.

Suhor, C. 1988. Content and process in the English curriculum. In *Content of the curriculum*. Edited by R. S. Brandt. Alexandria, Va.: Association for Supervision and Curriculum Development.

Taylor, O. 1990. *Cross-cultural communication: An essential dimension of effective education*. Washington, D.C.: The Mid-Atlantic Equity Center.

Tolar, D. O. 1992. My favorite newsteam: Comparative analysis of the nightly news. *The Speech Communication Teacher: Ideas and Strategies for Classrooms and Activities* 7 (1): 9.

Tough, J. 1979. *The development of meaning*. London: George Allen & Unwin Ltd.

Vygotsky, L. S. 1979. *Mind in society, the development of higher psychological processes*. Cambridge: Harvard University Press.

Wiggins, G. 1991. Standards, not standardization: Evoking quality student work. *Educational Leadership* 48 (5): 18–25.

Wittrock, M. C. 1983. Writing and the teaching of reading. Pp. 77–83 in *Composing and comprehending*. Edited by J. M. Jensen. Urbana, Ill.: ERIC/Educational Resources Information Center Clearinghouse on Reading and Comprehension Skills.

Wolff, F. I., N. C. Marsnick, W. S. Tacey, and R. G. Nichols. 1983. *Perceptive Listening*. New York: Holt, Rinehart & Winston.

Youngblood, E. 1985. Reading, thinking, and writing using the reading journal. *English Journal* 74: 46–48.

Zeuschner, R. 1993. *Communicating today*. Needham Heights, Mass.: Allyn and Bacon.

# DATE DUE

|  |  |  |  |
|---|---|---|---|
|  |  |  |  |
|  |  |  |  |
|  |  |  |  |
|  |  |  |  |
|  |  |  |  |
|  |  |  |  |
|  |  |  |  |
|  |  |  |  |
|  |  |  |  |
|  |  |  |  |
|  |  |  |  |
|  |  |  |  |
|  |  |  |  |
|  |  |  |  |
|  |  |  |  |
|  |  |  |  |
|  |  |  |  |
|  |  |  |  |
|  |  |  |  |
|  |  |  |  |
|  |  |  |  |